EXILES AND STRANGERS

EXILES
AND STRANGERS

A Reading of Camus's
Exile and the Kingdom

English Showalter, Jr.

Ohio State University Press : Columbus

Library of Congress Cataloguing in Publication Data:

Showalter, English

   Exiles and strangers

   Bibliography: p.
   Includes index.
   1. Camus, Albert, 1913–1960. Exil et le royaume.
I. Title.
PQ2605.A3734E938   1983   843'.914   83–12092
ISBN 0–8142–0353–1

For my father

CONTENTS

Acknowledgments

I would like to take this opportunity to express my thanks to Walter K. Gordon, dean of the Camden College of Arts and Sciences of Rutgers University, and provost of the Camden campus, for his continuous and generous encouragement and support of my work.

Some of the ideas in this book arose in my classes at Rutgers, Camden, and many were developed and clarified in discussions with students, who have become too numerous to name. Most of them are far from the academic world now, but I hope some at least may discover here my expression of appreciation for their contribution.

My best critic is, not surprisingly, my wife, Elaine. It is a rare advantage always to be able to discuss ideas with her and ask her advice on matters great and small. What I have learned from her over the years is incalculable, and I will not try to thank her for it here. She was, however, the first reader of the manuscript of this book, and much of what I like best in its final version she helped me put there. For that, at least, it is surely appropriate to acknowledge my gratitude in these pages.

EXILES AND STRANGERS

 One

Exile and the Kingdom and the American Reader

When Albert Camus was killed in an automobile accident on 4 January 1960, at the age of forty-six, he had already earned an international reputation, crowned by a Nobel Prize in 1957. The Swedish academy's award, however, had come as a shock to most people, even to the French who knew Camus best. Camus was the youngest writer ever to win it, except for Rudyard Kipling fifty years before, and his oeuvre was of rather modest size. Camus himself said he would have voted for André Malraux. Jean-Paul Sartre, who would later decline a Nobel Prize, had quarreled publicly with Camus, and much of the French Left followed Sartre in regarding Camus with suspicion, anger, or scorn in the late 1950s. In 1957, Camus was neither so well known nor so generally respected as he has been since his death.

The Nobel judges had nevertheless accurately sensed Camus's importance as an intellectual and moral leader, who, in the words of their citation, "illuminated the problems of the human conscience in our times."[1] In the two decades since his death, that judgment has been amply confirmed. His works are still widely read throughout the world. In France, *The Stranger* has sold more than four million copies, and more than three million in the United States.[2] Scholars and critics devote consistent attention to Camus; the Archives des Lettres Modernes series publishes an annual volume on him, there have been two international Camus symposia at the University of Florida, and the organizer of the 1980 gathering spoke accurately of "the unabated flow of books, articles, and essays on Camus."[3] Moreover, journalists and writers in the mass media still invoke him; on the occasion of a reissue of his *Notebooks* in 1978, a *Time* essayist wrote that "his formal works are as pertinent as the day they were written a world ago,"[4] and *Commentary*, in November 1980, carried an article on "The Posthumous Victory of Albert Camus."[5]

Despite the Nobel Prize, Camus's short career had been difficult and controversial, and never more so than in the last decade of his life. During World War II, Camus became celebrated in France for his heroic Resistance journalism, his brilliant first novel, *The Stranger* (1942), and his philosophical essay, *The Myth of Sisyphus* (1942). He also won the admiration and friendship of Sartre, and after the war the two men were cited together everywhere as the moral leaders of French youth, and less accurately as co-leaders of the Existentialist movement. Camus's productivity continued high; he published his second novel, *The Plague* (1947), and several volumes of plays and essays, leading up to *The Rebel* (1951). *The Rebel* precipitated the break with Sartre, who allowed an unfavorable review to be published in his journal *Les Temps modernes*; the review was followed by an exchange of rebuttals and counter-rebuttals. Intellectually, the break was unavoidable because Sartre had decided to accept the political leadership of the Soviet Communists, whose totalitarian policies were among those attacked by Camus in *The Rebel*; but on a personal level, Camus suffered acutely over the lost friendship. At the same time, the crisis over France's relationship with Algeria was growing more serious every day. Camus, who was born and raised in Algeria, refused to endorse any simple solution, to give unqualified support to either side, or to condone random violence in the name of justice; but his appeals for moderation went largely unheard and certainly unheeded. Ultimately, he felt constrained to adopt an attitude of silence, saying: "Between wisdom reduced to silence and madness which shouts itself hoarse, I prefer the virtues of silence."[6] On the part of the former hero of the Resistance, one of the great advocates of commitment, this statement clearly denotes a time of despair. The early 1950s had also been a period of extended literary sterility.

In 1956, Camus produced *The Fall*, his first major work since *The Rebel*. As one would expect, it was greeted with mixed critical responses; but much of the hostile criticism was tainted with ideological bias. *The Fall* was a great success with the public not only in France but in the United States, where it stayed twelve weeks on the bestseller lists in early 1957. Even to denigrators, *The Fall* seemed to signal a renewal of Camus's creative energy. The stories of *Exile and the Kingdom* were completed and published in one volume the next year; they were to be Camus's last book. Once again, critics were divided, but the public enthusiastic.

In the United States, five of the six stories had appeared first in mass-circulation magazines: *The Adulterous Woman* in *Mademoiselle* in January 1958; *The Renegade* in the *Partisan Review*, winter 1958; *The Silent Men* in *Vogue*, December 1957; *The Guest* in the *Atlantic Monthly*, December 1957; the *The Growing Stone* in *Esquire*, February 1958. The complete volume, *Exile and the Kingdom*, was published in early 1958. It received a page-one review in the *New York Times Book Review* on 9 March and climbed onto the bestseller list for eight weeks from 31 March to 18 May. The book was widely reviewed in the American press, with widely disparate reactions and considerable disagreement over the merits of individual stories.[7] Most of the reviewers liked *The Guest* and *The Renegade* best, although *Time*'s anonymous critic ranked *The Artist at Work* first, and Ramon Guthrie thought *The Adulterous Woman* showed the "restraint and precision that characterize Camus's best work," whereas "by contrast, *The Renegade* seems raucous and inept." Norman Podhoretz was virtually alone in terming *The Guest* "the weakest of the stories." After more leisurely reading than the first reviewers could afford, and consideration in the context of Camus's complete works, *The Renegade* and *The Guest* would probably still be ranked highest; but all six stories have elicited admiration and serious study, and most readers would agree with judgments like John Cruickshank's "[Camus] achieved an outstanding measure of moral and artistic integrity which perhaps reached their culminating point in his third novel, *La Chute* (1956), and in the short stories—which are also a set of fascinating stylistic exercises—collected under the title *L'Exil et le royaume* (1957)."[8]

The public, in Camus's case, had been ahead of the critics and the literary journalists. Despite the fact that *The Fall* had stayed on the bestseller lists for twelve weeks in early 1957, when Camus won the Nobel Prize in October, the media obviously thought they had to explain who Camus was. *Life*, which must have been tipped in advance, ran three pages of pictures of Camus and his family under the title "Action-Packed Intellectual."[9] *Newsweek* wrote: "Scarcely more than a decade ago, the name of Albert Camus was almost unknown outside the hurly-burly of Parisian literary wars. On the basis of his first novel (*The Stranger*, published in the U.S. in 1946), he was considered merely another minor facet of the French existentialist movement dominated by his more spectacular friend Jean-Paul Sartre."[10] A *New York Times* editorialist similarly remarked that Camus began as "an existentialist who subscribed to the philosophy that human life was absurd and futile, but he outgrew the existentialist movement"; and on the news pages, the profile of Camus concluded with the information, "The writer's name is pronounced Al-BAIR Kam-EUE."[11]

Since coverage of Camus was suddenly timely, a different sort of testimony also began filtering through. Justin O'Brien, Camus's translator but also a professor at Columbia, commented in January 1958: "At the present moment about 70 percent of our brightest French majors in colleges and universities are impelled to communicate some special message about Camus."[12] In the same month, in an article in *Catholic World* entitled "Albert Camus: Guide of a Generation," Thomas Molnar claimed that "nine students out of ten, if asked to name a contemporary author with the greatest impact on youth, will mention Albert Camus in the first place."[13] By the time of his death, only two years later, Camus's immense popularity had been recognized; a *New York Times* editorial referred to "an almost worshipful following among the younger intellectuals and among youth in general, both in France and abroad."[14] Five years later, "Genêt" said in the *New Yorker*, "Camus has now become the idol of young French readers."[15] and in 1968, as the ferment over Vietnam approached a climax, Lionel Abel, on the say-so of a graduate student at the State University of New York at Buffalo, placed Camus in a pantheon of "Seven Heroes of the New Left," the others being Paul Goodman, Noam Chomsky, Che Guevara, Régis Debray, Franz Fanon, and Herbert Marcuse.[16]

Many American students must have made their first acquaintance with Camus as the author of one of the stories in *Exile and the Kingdom*. Almost from the moment of their first publication, they began to appear in anthologies, most of which were intended for use as textbooks. *The Guest* has appeared in at least seventeen different English-language anthologies. *The Adulterous Woman* has also been very popular, and was included in the classic *Understanding Fiction*, by Cleanth Brooks and Robert Penn Warren.[17] *The Renegade* and *The Growing Stone* have each been anthologized at least once. The stories have also been published frequently in French, in anthologies intended for language classes. *Exile and the Kingdom* has thus been one of Camus's most widely disseminated works in America.

It was also the last major work published before Camus's untimely death. In view of his continued popularity, and the strong scholarly and critical interest in his works, *Exile and the Kingdom* ought logically to have attracted an unusual amount of attention. Instead, the opposite has been true. The nature of the work, obviously, poses a problem; a collection of six independent stories can seldom have the powerful impact of a single unified narrative of equal length. Even the most enthusiastic reviewers tended to find fault with some of the stories thereby not only reducing the stature of the book, but implying that its structure and message were fragmentary.

The message, moreover, as it was originally perceived, may well have displeased some of Camus's admirers; Bernard Murchland, writing for *Catholic World*, said admiringly and accurately, "But in *The Fall* (1956) and his recent collection of stories, *Exile and the Kingdom*, he stresses the new values of penance and expiation. The theme of transcendence, the creative value of suffering and human solidarity are added to the Camusian vision."[18] Those who most appreciated in Camus his nihilistic vision or his Mediterranean paganism did not welcome this evolution; and since Camus did not live to carry it to its conclusion, many critics still prefer to ignore it. *The Fall*, which cannot be ignored, is sufficiently ambiguous to allow other readings more consistent with the image of a coherent oeuvre, bringing closure to a cycle rather than opening onto a speculative future.

Whatever the reason, *Exile and the Kingdom* has been greatly neglected by comparison with *The Stranger*, *The Plague*, and *The Fall*. The first authoritative biography of Camus, written—not surprisingly—by an American, Herbert Lottman, and published in 1979, scarcely mentions *Exile and the Kingdom* in its more than seven hundred meticulously documented pages.[19] Most general studies of Camus do likewise. Although there have been a substantial number of articles and one book on *Exile and the Kingdom*, a great deal remains to be said about it. Peter Cryle's *Bilan critique: "L'Exil et le royaume" d'Albert Camus, essai d'analyse* (1973) provides a useful point of departure, since it summarizes all the criticism up to 1972; Cryle wrote then that "in-depth studies of it are rare, and the few there are are not very satisfactory."[20] Cryle's work is now almost a decade old; more articles have appeared, but no more in-depth studies. Cryle devotes a good deal of his effort to discussing the unity of the collection, and to good purpose, since its diversity may have been an obstacle to its acceptance as a major work. I will not return to this question, which I think Cryle and others have adequately treated. Camus undeniably meant to suggest some thematic unity when he gave the collection its title. The same themes appear elsewhere in Camus, and indeed elsewhere in modern literature; but we may suppose a particular coherence of vision in six stories composed at about the same time and published together by their author. In other words, I assume a coherence of vision, and refer to it when it is relevant to my own point; but my purpose lies in another area. For the stories were conceived, written, and published separately, and continue to be read in most cases isolated from each other, especially by Americans, who still make up one of Camus's most devoted audiences.

Camus has been termed so often "the spokesman of his generation and the conscience of his epoch"—the phrase is from Justin O'Brien and Léon Roudiez,[21] but there are similar ones in almost every article written since his death—that the real sources of his popularity with American readers, especially young ones, have become obscured. Theodore Solatoroff remarked wittily in 1968: ". . . If [Camus] speaks now from the grave, as he does virtually every day, it is usually in this way: to confer some sort of nobility on other men's positions or prose. His reputation seems more or less honorific. . . ."[22] In the mid 1960s, "Genêt" quoted French students as saying that "what they desire and obtain from his books is a sense of morality without religion. They are touched by what they identify as his romanticism, that is, his connection with violent situations in modern history."[23] The mythical Camus implied in these broad venerations was a man who brought clarity to difficult issues, provided reason and reasons, who made sense without sacrificing truth or humanity. Camus's style tends to support that impression; deliberately simple in syntax, restrained in vocabulary, often colloquial, what Roland Barthes called "transparent" or "neutral,"[24] Camus's language seems to provide the reader with direct access to a familiar reality.

Barthes, of course, describes this illusion only to denounce it, and much of the critical writing on Camus has been devoted to revealing his hidden complexities. The first reviewers in America noticed a tension between some superficial clarity and a profound, pervasive ambiguity. Orville Prescott, a regular reviewer for the daily *New York Times*, was outraged:

> It is M. Camus's failure as an artist that he ignores "the greatest number of men" and writes ambiguous and symbolical parables. . . . Most short stories are either stories in the old-fashioned sense or they are studies of character, emotion and the meaning of particular behavior or circumstances. Both kinds require a minimum of lucidity in communication. But M. Camus's short stories are

beautifully written and highly suggestive puzzles. Any reader can interpret them to suit himself. The professor's answer is no more likely to be correct than the freshman student's. This kind of short fiction, no matter how morally earnest—and M. Camus's stories are written with deadly earnestness—can only be a sort of fashionable, intellectual game to be enjoyed by a small coterie. When cryptic hints and solemn posturing become the substance of fiction, life itself is drained from it. The six stories in *Exile and the Kingdom* are all riddles in the reader's path.

Prescott goes on to describe three of the stories and to articulate some of the riddles: "Riddle: in what symbolical fashion was the woman adulterous? . . . Answers are not easy. I can think of several; but thinking of them is a dull way of wasting time and a story like this seems to me a sterile and tiresome performance."[25] Real professors, who read this story in *Understanding Fiction* and discussed it with real freshmen, were surely less disturbed by its ambiguities than Prescott, and one can only laugh at the description of Camus's millions of readers as "a small coterie." Prescott was regularly hostile to Camus in his reviews, and reading his obtuse attacks brings back to life the atmosphere in which Camus seemed to young readers an anti-Establishment rebel and nonconformist crusader.

The same tension was often singled out for criticism by more sympathetic and more perceptive reviewers, however. Bernard Murchland, a consistent admirer, nonetheless qualified his praise by saying, "In *Exile and the Kingdom*, Camus never quite escapes a quality of indeterminateness that ill befits his creative ability and what seems to be his intention. . . . There is a curious discrepancy between Camus's technical excellence and intensity and the final rather vague evaluation his characters make of their own dilemmas."[26] Norman Podhoretz said that the final pages of *The Stranger* "remain unclear even after several rereadings," and that several of the stories in *Exile and the Kingdom* "involve the same conflict between the nihilistic imagination that broods compulsively on death, executions, sickness, and doom, and the intellect seeking reasons to refute the evidence dredged up by the imagination. And these stories have the same peculiarity as the novel: they end in obscurity."[27] Both Podhoretz and Murchland describe perceptively one aspect of Camus's stories, but they condemn a basic device of Camus's art, one that many readers have found a strongly positive quality.

In fact, this very quality seems to me one of the reasons for Camus's durable and general popularity. He seems to be making sense—about murky, insoluble, real problems. Where there is obscurity, it is admitted as a difficulty not just for the reader but also for the character and implicitly for the author. Camus's stories always end on a note of perplexity and virtually demand that the reader formulate extensions beyond the text, into real plausibility—into our world, not his fictional construct.

In discussing the stories individually, I have in most cases taken up some obvious "riddles," a surprising number of which have not only never been answered but apparently not even asked. The nature of Janine's adultery, tiresome and dull though the subject seemed to Orville Prescott, has been thoroughly discussed; yet no one seems to have wondered what Camus's *Adulterous Woman* might owe to the biblical story from which he took the title and the symbol. No one has discussed the symbolic function of the barrels in *The Silent Men* or the role of the policeman in *The Growing Stone*. In *The Artist at Work*, critics have returned again and again to the story of Jonah and the whale, without considering the rest of the Book of Jonah. From such specific problems, I have worked toward a coherent reading of each story, following a personal and empirical sense of what signified in each one, and incorporating eclectically whatever methods seemed useful. I have willingly acceded to Camus's pressure to examine some of the ethical implications of his writing; readers continue to find them exciting and rewarding after a quarter of a century.

All six stories turn on moral themes that remain quite timely. In the current idiom, they deal with women's liberation, extremism, labor relations, terrorism, privacy, and modernization, respectively. Janine, "the adulterous woman," recognizes her husband's limitations and the stifling effects of her marriage. Orville Prescott described her, with unforgiving accuracy, as "irritable, bored, stupid, scornful of her husband, frightened of life."[28] She has become a stock character as a feminist protagonist. The Renegade cannot stand uncertainty and compromise; the inevitable outcome of his logic is to become an assassin. The desert setting is almost surrealistic, but the Renegade's way of thinking has become an everyday reality. Daru, in *The Guest*, is a French Algerian, a would-be moderate in a situation poisoned by the past. With irrational violence the political tactic of both sides, an individual's virtue provides no protection and no escape. Yvars and his co-workers, "the silent men," are skilled laborers in an obsolescent industry. They are the victims of progress, not because of poverty and material deprivation, but because of their broken pride and the disruption of their lives. Jonas, the artist, cannot successfully combine his fame with his private life, especially his family.[29] D'Arrast, in the final story, is a French engineer who comes to build a levee in an isolated Brazilian village. He might be a Peace Corpsman, a United Nations worker, or a "technical adviser." His problem, not obvious at first, is to prevent his own idealism from blinding him to the limited possibilities inherent in the situation.

It is, in short, easy to find relevance in the subjects. It would betray the stories to reduce any one of them to no more than a timely topic; and Camus has no practical advice to offer in any case. I believe these themes are actually paradigmatic enough to remain pertinent for a long time to come, and I do not think a miraculous social revolution would render them meaningless, any more than antibiotics have eliminated *The Plague* along with the plague. For American readers, the manner in which Camus approaches the dilemmas of real life is probably more important than the dilemma itself. His characters are typically unexceptional people, whose good intentions and reasonable expectations come to grief because of overwhelming natural, historical, political, economic, or social forces. The central characters repeat a plaintive, "Nothing turned out as I expected"; and yet they cannot identify villains or even fix on a mistake of their own. This version of the individual's alienation is very familiar to Americans, all of us schooled, like Camus, as liberal humanists, suspicious of doctrines and trusting of people, even our adversaries.

Janine is trapped because even after her revelation she feels need and affection for Marcel. Yvars understands his boss's difficulties as well as his own. Daru has as much sympathy, and as much revulsion, for the prisoner as for the policeman. Jonas loves Louise, his children, Rateau, his art, his circle of friends, his busy life, all too equally for his time and ability. The Renegade and D'Arrast are somewhat different cases. The Renegade suppresses any doubts in himself by force and adopts the severest discipline of Catholicism because he is tempted by food, women, and pleasure. His fate, when he meets a stronger faith than his own, is to be destroyed. His rejection of liberal humanism seems worse than the others' acceptance of it. D'Arrast, on the other hand, appears to represent the hope that humanism may yet prevail. D'Arrast succeeds at all levels, brings material aid, finds spiritual brotherhood despite his skepticism, maintains good relations with the poor and with the ruling class. One shudders to imagine this story as Graham Greene might have written it. We must remember, however, that *The Growing Stone* is only one of six stories, and reserve judgment on its implications for Camus's general beliefs until we have looked at it more closely.

The more usual pattern, which is full of resonances with our own lives and times, is that the characters cannot decide whom to sacrifice to the general welfare, and so they sacrifice themselves, chiefly by doing nothing. They succumb to a sort of moral paralysis. They began their lives with a naive optimism that if they did their jobs, avoided trouble, and lived normally, everything would work out all right and they would be happy. Jonas even invokes that symbol of providential guidance, his star. The United States was founded on that Enlightenment optimism which held that in the long run the individual's welfare was identical to the universal welfare; and it is a myth we still hold dear. So like Candide, we rush after the newest avatar of El Dorado, careering from crisis to crisis along the way. Practical politics is concerned with taking actions, distributing resources, assigning obligations. Every action taken, every solution to every problem, creates a new problem somewhere else within the system. Ultimately, when an actual choice must be made, the lesser of two evils is often not lesser enough for people of principle to endorse in good conscience. At that point, they succumb to paralysis and fall silent. Camus understood only too well the dilemma of the liberal humanist in the real world. He himself was finally reduced to inaction and silence over the Algerian question, and he said poignantly of his decision, "When speech manages to dispose without remorse of the existence of others, to remain silent is not a negative attitude."[30]

I have touched on these questions of relevance and moral application to the present because I think they help explain the receptivity of American readers to Camus's works. There is an instant identification, a response that requires no prompting from critics or pedagogues. I have, then, written with American readers very much in mind, for three reasons: because they constitute a large and devoted audience, because I belong to that audience myself and am sensitive to its interests, and because Camus responds exceptionally well to those interests. I should emphasize, however, that Americans are by no means alone in appreciating Camus. Major criticism of *Exile and the Kingdom* has come from Australia, Canada, England, and Germany, as well as France and the United States. It will soon be clear that most of the critical approaches to Camus have already provoked international discussion and debate. I hope and expect that my readings will have value for all of Camus's diverse and far-flung audience. A critic as much as an author must proceed from personal concerns and local sources. I have explained mine in order to clarify my methods and purposes, not to restrict their application or to exclude any readers.

Addressing an Anglophone audience has, however, dictated an important choice in presentation: I have written in English myself, and in the text I have used English translations of the French, giving the original in footnotes.[31] Where any significant difference exists, I have called attention to it. In addition, I have devoted an appendix to the translation as a whole, in an effort to evaluate its overall accuracy, and to show in general rather than in fragmentary detail how the translation differs from the original.

Camus's relevance and moral concern, which provide the initial basis for many readers' sympathy, have never really been challenged, even by Camus's enemies. Rather, at least with regard to his fiction, his art has been attacked, for a lack of subtlety and depth, or for a failure to match its techniques to its ends. Accordingly, the central questions I take up in each case are literary, not political or ethical. In *The Adulterous Woman*, it is primarily a matter of structure; in *The Renegade*, the narrative point of view; in *The Silent Men*, symbolism; in *The Guest*, ambiguity; in *The Artist at Work*, irony; and in *The Growing Stone*, the concluding function of the story. Camus was a writer, not a philosopher or a legislator. The moral and political purposes he intended his writing to serve are best fulfilled by critical reading. What terrified Orville Prescott has in a sense come true: the freshman student's interpretation may be as good as the professor's; Camus intended it so. For the purpose is not to find the answer to the riddle but to learn to look for it. Even seniors are still willing to accept some guidance on that, and the purpose of my work is to raise some of the central questions and to propose some models of response.

In the final chapter, I have considered *Exile and the Kingdom* in its entirety, not as a structural unity, but as the best evidence we have of Camus's moral vision in his last years. Ironically, as an ending to his life's work, *Exile and the Kingdom* seems a kind of anticlimactic epilogue, like the dénouements of the stories, leaving the reader with the same kind of perplexity. Something obviously is not finished; a change is in progress, but the ultimate outcome can only be guessed at. This chapter at least begins to remedy the neglect of *Exile and the Kingdom* as a signficant part of Camus's lifework. I have traced some of the important continuities, which are also paths of significant differences, from *The Stranger* to *Exile and the Kingdom*. In calling this chapter "Camus's Last Words," I have meant to emphasize the irony; for if they are last chronologically, they are not definitive. Indeed, it does not seem to me that Camus ever expected to make a definitive statement. The point of his stories is never an answer to the unanswerable question, never a solution to the insoluble problem, never an escape from the eternal dilemma. It is, rather, an appeal to confront the truth in a world that dictates many unpalatable answers, furnishes unacceptable solutions, and offers ony illusory escapes. From that confrontation with the truth, however, there may yet come hope, the will to persevere, and the possibility of happiness.

1. Quoted in Lottman, *Albert Camus*, p. 607.

2. The figures for France come from Abbou et al., "Albert Camus, vingt ans après," *Les Nouvelles Litté*raires, 10–17 January 1980, pp. 18–19. The figures on American sales were kindly given to me by the publisher, Random House.

3. Gay-Crosier, *Albert Camus 1980*, p. vii.

4. Stefan Kanfer, "Camus," *Time*, 10 July 1978, pp. 74–75.

5. By Stephen Miller, pp. 53–58.

6. Quoted in Lottman, *Albert Camus*, p. 626.

7. The following reviews are mentioned in this passage: Richard G. Davis, *New York Times Book Review*, 9 March 1958, p. 1; Ramon Guthrie, *New York Herald-Tribune Book Review*, 9 March 1958, p. 3; *Time*, 17 March 1958, p. 111; Norman Podhoretz, *New Yorker*, 29 March 1958, pp. 115–22.

8. "French Literature since 1870," in D. G. Charlton, ed., *France: A Companion to French Studies*, p. 422.

9. *Life*, 14 October 1957, pp. 125–28; the news of the award came on 18 October.

10. "The Startled Winner," 28 October 1957, pp. 50–51.

11. "Nobel Prize Winner," 19 October 1957, p. 20; "Albert Camus Wins Nobel Letters Prize," 18 October 1957, p. 8.

12. "An Entry in Camus' Bibliography." Review of Maquet's *Albert Camus, the Invincible Summer*, *New York Times Book Review*, 5 January 1958, p. 14.

13. P. 272.

14. "Albert Camus," 5 January 1960, p. 4.

15. 6 February 1965, pp. 115–16.

16. *New York Times Magazine*, 5 May 1968, pp. 30 ff.

17. In the second edition, 1959–79; it has been replaced in the third edition.

18. "Albert Camus: Rebel," January 1959, p. 312.

19. *Albert Camus, a Biography*.

20. P. 7: "Les études approfondies en sont rares, et le peu qu'il y en a sont assez peu satisfaisantes."

21. "Camus," *Saturday Review*, 13 February 1960, p. 19.

22. "Camus' Portable Pedestal," *New Republic*, 21 December 1968, p. 27.

23. *New Yorker*, 6 February 1965, p. 115.

24. *Le Degré zéro de l'écriture*, pp. 109–10.

25. "Books of the Times: *Exile and the Kingdom*," 10 March 1958, p. 21.

26. "One Step Further on a Solitary Way," *Commonweal*, 28 March 1958, pp. 663–64.

27. *New Yorker*, 29 March 1958, p. 115.

28. *New York Times*, 10 March 1958, p. 21.

29. "At 43, Camus lives in Paris and jealously guards his personal privacy—relaxing his restrictions for these exclusive *Life* photographs," according to "Action-Packed Intellectual," *Life*, 14 October 1957, p. 115; perhaps the first sitting for "The Artist at Work"?

30. Quoted in Lottman, *Albert Camus*, p. 626.

31. See the bibliography for information on the editions used.

 Two

The Adulterous Woman:
New Forms of Judgment

The Adulterous Woman relates a day in the life of Janine, a woman in her forties who has accompanied her husband Marcel, a cloth merchant, on a business trip south into Algeria. The narration is in the third person, but limited to Janine's point of view. The story begins on a bus, which arrives at an oasis town around midday. Janine and Marcel settle in their hotel room, walk through the town to visit the local merchants, go up late in the day onto the parapet of a fort, where Janine has intimations of a freedom she has only vaguely been aware of before, and then go back to the hotel. During the night, Janine returns to the fort, where she has another, more powerful experience, sensing her own place in the eternal wheeling of the stars. This moment of revelation, described in highly erotic terms, ends with the line "the whole sky stretched out over her, fallen on her back on the cold earth" (33).[1] She then returns to her husband. Obviously, the adultery promised by the title is purely symbolic.

Two questions seem to arise from this story. First of all, what is the exact nature of Janine's experience at the fort? Did Camus, that is to say, mean for us to recognize this as a mystical revelation, a literary epiphany, or a psychological breakdown? Second, what is the significance of the cryptic final paragraph? Janine gets back into bed, apparently without Marcel's knowing she was gone; but he awakens a moment later, says something Janine does not understand, goes to the bathroom for a drink of mineral water, and is about to slip into bed again when "he

looked at her, without understanding. She was weeping copiously, unable to restrain herself. 'It's nothing, dear,' she said, 'it's
nothing'" (33).[2] To some readers, this amounts to an authentic
reconciliation with reality; to others, it signals a permanent loss
of the "kingdom" and return to exile. Such endings are typical of
Camus's stories, and obviously, Camus intended the reader not
to know the answer.

Thus, this apparently simple story, like the life it tells,
contains some mysteries. In order to read them intelligibly, we
must replace them in the context of the entire narrative sequence, and see how Camus builds to the climax on the parapet,
what is resolved there, and what remains after Janine's return to
the hotel room. Ostensibly, most of the story follows the very
routine events of the day, and sets within that framework
Janine's random thoughts and reminiscences. But the routine
sales trip turns out to have a hidden pattern, at least as Janine
perceives it; and the random ideas it evokes keep returning
obsessively to a small number of themes, which eventually
coalesce into a single clear pattern.[3]

Time is one of the broadest structuring concepts in human
consciousness. In the beginning of *The Adulterous Woman*, the
hours of the day are recorded with some regularity. By evening,
a more general sense of time replaces the clock-watching
chronology, preparing us for one important aspect of Janine's
revelation, the experience of eternity through the infinite ex-
pansion of the moment. The latter kind of time has, however,
been present all along. We learn with precision that "the bus had
left only at dawn" and that "for two hours in the cold morning it
had been advancing," but we read in the same passage that "it
seemed to her as if she had been traveling for days" (5).[4] A
similar temporal disorientation occurs in the next paragraph,
this time concerning Janine's entire life: "Was that so long ago?
Twenty-five years. Twenty-five years were nothing, for it seemed
to her only yesterday . . ."[5] In short, though Janine remains
quite capable of reading the calendar or the clock, she makes the
effort to do so primarily because, from the outset, she feels a
discrepancy between real and felt time, between chronology and
duration.

Besides the twin confusions about time, there are many hints
that the journey, at least the bus trip, is a recapitulation of
Janine's entire life. For example, at the start of the ride, the sky
was clear and the horizon visible; but the wind-whipped sand
had shrouded the bus until they "were silently progressing in a
sort of sleepless night" (5).[6] A few paragraphs later, remem-
bering her married life, Janine thinks: "The years had passed in
the semi-darkness behind the half-closed shutters. Summer, the
beaches, excursions, the mere sight of the sky were things of the
past" (8).[7] A recurrent theme in Janine's reverie is summed up in
the sentence, "No, nothing had happened as she had expected"
(7).[8] In the context, following on an interruption caused by the
bus's honking and Janine's sudden awareness of a French soldier
across the aisle, it is hard to say exactly to what this sentence
refers. On the one hand, it fits her marriage: Marcel has
provided neither the companionship nor the security she expected. On the other hand, it fits the trip; she had anticipated
"heat, the swarms of flies, the filthy hotels . . . palm trees, soft
sand" (9)[9] and finds none of these—although it is a fly, "an odd
sight here" (3)[10] and therefore a reminder of her expectations,
that sets off Janine's train of thought in the first line of the story.
I could pursue the analogy of marriage and journey to include
the bus's stalling, Marcel's stolid presence beside Janine, the
couple's isolation from the other passengers, and so on. Critics
have noticed a comparable device in the second story, where the
Renegade's life parallels the day he spends waiting for the
missionary. It is, in both cases, not a literal incident-by-incident
transposition, but rather a general feeling of convergence of the
life in the past with the present.

When, therefore, Janine goes up to the fort at night, her new
experience of time comes not as an unexpected revelation but as
the resolution of a problem of which she herself had been aware,
if only dimly. Both chronology and duration are submerged in
her identification with a vaster time, that of eternity: "She was
turning with them [the stars] and the apparently stationary
progress little by little identified her with the core of her being"
(32).[11] Time, which is in part an objective phenomenon, independent of the fiction but used by Camus to confer a classical

unity on *The Adulterous Woman,* is also a theme of the
heroine's growing self-awareness, which is the principal structuring element of the story.

The natural correlate of time is, of course, space. Janine feels
her contact with the physical world about her in ways parallel to
her sense of time. The progress of the bus across the desert and
the walk around the town pose no problems; these are the
objective measures, the equivalents to clock time and the calendar. Nonetheless, as we have seen, the fog and blowing sand
obscure the horizon for part of the day. This spatial disorientation is developed in a series of problematic encounters with the
material world.

To begin with the most literal, Janine has always felt herself to
be somewhat large; Marcel is "a little shorter than she" (6).[12] On
the bus, the Arabs seem to have plenty of room in their seats,
"where she and her husband felt wedged in" (7)[13]—and so she
pulls her coat tighter about her. As they set out after lunch, she
"would have liked to take up less space" (16).[14] Coming down
from the first trip to the fort, "she felt too tall, too thick" (25).[15]
Her weight makes the bed rattle. On her way back to the fort,
however, she encounters three Arabs on bicycles, and they have
"vast burnooses" (31);[16] moreover, instead of trying to shrink
from them, she stands her ground and lets the burnooses brush
against her. On the parapet, she forgets not only the destructive
passing of time but "the weight of beings" (32).[17]

Janine's sense of her physical being takes in much more than
her bigness, however; her size is just part of a complex of
associations. As a girl, she had "won the first prize in gymnastics
and hadn't known what it was to be winded" (5–6),[18] yet she
cannot bend down to check Marcel's sample case under the bus
seat. In the hotel room, she feels the heaviness of her legs; and
during the afternoon, she grows weary walking. When she goes
to the fort at night, however, she runs the entire distance.

Throughout the early part of the story, Janine suffers from the
cold. One of her earliest thoughts was, "The weather was cold"
(3);[19] and one of her disenchantments with the trip is that "she
had not thought of the cold, of the biting wind, of these
semipolar plateaux" (9).[20] Upon arriving at the oasis, she sees

the palm trees, "and she would have liked to go toward them. But although it was close to noon, the cold was bitter; the wind made her shiver" (13).[21] She goes to her room instead. During the first visit to the fort, however, it is Marcel who feels the cold and the fatigue; and when Janine returns by night, "breathing deeply, she forgot the cold" (32).[22]

Her eating and drinking follow the same course. On the bus, the French soldier gives her a lozenge, which she takes hesitantly. It is a disappointment, however, for she thinks of it as an overture to something more; but the soldier does not even notice her afterward. The noon meal she eats with Marcel—pork and wine—"bothered her somewhat" (16).[23] After their evening meal, both she and Marcel, exhausted, silent, sick, drag themselves to their icy room and sleep. Back at the fort, however, Janine finds her proper nourishment: "The cold air she was gulping down flowed evenly inside her and a spark of warmth began to glow amidst her shivers" (31–32);[24] and it is the pure water of night that fills and satisfies her.

Camus has then provided an extensive range of physical sensations, all of which evolve simultaneously in the same way, and which reflect the same changing self-awareness as the sense of time. Much the most important of Janine's physical senses, however, is her sexuality. Despite the title of the story, and the unmistakably erotic language of the climax, critics have been singularly blind to this theme. The French soldier on the bus seems to initiate an ordinary seduction, but nothing comes of it at all. He serves to emphasize the symbolic nature of Janine's adultery, as others have pointed out. This need not imply, however, that real sexuality plays no important role in the story, for in fact it returns constantly in Janine's thoughts.

When Janine first notices the French soldier, she thinks that he is ogling her, and she blushes. Not long afterward, she feels too big for the seat, and consoles herself with the reflection: "Yet she wasn't so fat—tall and well rounded rather, plump and still desirable, as she was well aware when men looked at her" (7).[25] Yet at that very moment, her husband was "looking straight ahead"[26]—perhaps not significant in a couple married for twenty-five years; but the soldier also, after having offered

Janine the lozenge, turned to "staring at the road, straight in front of him" (12).[27] When they arrive at the oasis, outside the hotel, she "saw the soldier coming toward her. She was expecting him to smile or salute. He passed without looking at her and disappeared" (13).[28] On the street in the late afternoon, Janine "had never seen so many men. Yet none of them looked at her" (21).[29] They are all, to be sure, Arabs, and racial barriers would tend to make Janine invisible to them; but like Marcel, like the soldier, Janine has noticed them, and notices their failure to look at her.

Lying awake before her visit to the fort, Janine faces the truth about her sexuality:

> They made love in the dark, by feel, without seeing each other. Is there another love than that of darkness, a love that would cry aloud in daylight? She didn't know, but she did know that Marcel needed her, and that she needed that need, that she lived on it night and day, at night especially—every night, when he didn't want to be alone, or to age and die, with that set expression he assumed which she occasionally recognized on other men's faces, the only common expression of those madmen hiding under an appearance of wisdom until the madness seizes them and hurls them desperately toward a woman's body to bury in it, without desire, everything terrifying that solitude and night reveal to them" (27–28).[30]

Yet this particular night, "Marcel came to join her [in bed] and put the light out without asking anything of her" (26).[31] It would be too strong to assert categorically that Janine is no longer sexually desirable, but the day has certainly given her cause to doubt her desirability. At every turn, she has been ignored by men, in many cases where she needed, and indeed expected, to be desired. The eroticism of her experience at the fort is no mere trick of style. Janine has been preoccupied with sex throughout the story, but in much the same way as with the other themes of her thoughts. Sexuality, too, has disappointed her expectations, but she discovers an entirely new resolution of the problem in her orgasmic union with the night sky.

To sum up the structure, Camus has interwoven many themes in Janine's consciousness—time, her body, sexuality—all of which evolve in a roughly similar pattern. On the bus, she gradually becomes aware of them; in the town, they return to plague her, especially after she has the inkling of a solution during her first visit to the fort; finally, during her night visit, all of them are resolved in some fashion. The nature of the resolution depends, of course, on how one interprets the end of the story, when she returns to the hotel room; but before discussing an interpretation, I want to consider another clue Camus has given about his intentions.

Some of the stories in *Exile and the Kingdom* seem to be reworkings of earlier writings by Camus himself, but the collection owes very little to literary sources. *The Adulterous Woman* in particular has some affinities with *Noces*, "Retour à Tipasa," and *La Mort heureuse*,[32] but otherwise appears to be composed of materials drawn from real-life observation. Yet the title bluntly announces a literary debt, which, with astonishing unanimity, critics have ignored, or worse yet, dismissed; Jean Onimus called the story "a humorous tale, beginning with the title itself."[33] True, at first glance the comparison holds little promise. In Camus's version, the woman commits no actual adultery, nobody accuses her, and so nobody passes any judgment on her. To be sure, the familiar moral of the biblical story—"He that is without sin among you, let him first cast a stone at her" (John 8:7)—agrees with Camus's own thinking, at least in broad terms; but it is hard to see how it applies to Camus's story. On closer examination, however, we will see that there are many subtle connections.

The original version, in John 8:3–11 reads:

> And the scribes and Pharisees brought unto him a woman taken in adultery; and when they had set her in the midst,
> They say unto him, Master, this woman was taken in adultery, in the very act.
> Now Moses in the law commanded us, that such should be stoned: but what sayest thou?
> This they said, tempting him, that they might have to accuse him. But Jesus stooped down, and with his finger wrote on the ground, as though he heard them not.
> So when they continued asking him, he lifted up himself, and said unto them, He that is without sin among you, let him first cast a stone at her.

> And again he stooped down, and wrote on the ground.
>
> And they which heard it, being convicted by their own conscience, went out one by one, beginning at the eldest, even unto the last: and Jesus was left alone, and the woman standing in the midst.
>
> When Jesus had lifted up himself, and saw none but the woman, he said unto her, Woman, where are those thine accusers? hath no man condemned thee?
>
> She said, No man, Lord. And Jesus said unto her, Neither do I condemn thee: go, and sin no more.[34]

Most of the story is familiar to everyone, but the seemingly irrelevant detail of Jesus' writing on the ground is so seldom recalled as to be the most striking element. This writing must represent the new law of Jesus, based on love and mercy, which is to replace the old law of Moses, based on retribution. Moreover, whereas Moses went up onto the mountain to bring back the central articles of his law, Jesus lowers himself to deliver his. They are written upon the earth itself, suggesting the importance of the material Creation to the God who has made himself man. Accordingly, Jesus has each man look within himself for the law.

In Camus's story, Janine sees writing on the earth during her first visit to the fort: "All around them a flock of motionless dromedaries, tiny at that distance, formed against the gray ground the black signs of a strange handwriting, the meaning of which had to be deciphered" (23).[35] The strange script can thus be partly deciphered as an intertextual reference that explicitly associates Janine's adventure to the theme of law and judgment.[36]

Camus, of course, brings no god into his story; rather, the universe itself is the writing and the meaning. But just as adultery brought the biblical woman before Jesus, where she learned the new law, so too Janine's symbolic adultery will force her to reencounter the world and to ask herself profound questions about its meaning. Ultimately, the adulteress must face her conscience alone. In the beginning, the scribes and Pharisees bring her against her will into the middle of the crowd of men in the temple, where Jesus was. In similar fashion, Janine has been reluctantly brought on this journey by her husband, and she finds herself alone in a throng of men: "Not a single woman could be seen, and it seemed to Janine that she had never seen so many men" (21).[37] These alien men, accusers, lawgivers, judges, and, in Janine's case, supporters and protectors, too, cannot take the place of the woman's own responsibility for herself. Jesus' indirect rebuke to the scribes and Pharisees is not the final point of the story; in the end, he tells the woman that she also must judge herself. Camus has emphasized that ending, replacing the concern about law and judgment with a concern for human freedom and individual responsibility.

Stone is so much a part of Camus's world that one might easily overlook its function as an allusion. Mosaic law called for adulterous women to be stoned, however, and the scribes and Pharisees specifically recall that punishment to Jesus, who repeats the citation in his famous reply. Reading the Gospel account with Camus in mind, we can easily see how well the stones fit into Camus's symbolic landscape. Indeed, the Ten Commandments were inscribed on stone, in contrast to the earth on which Jesus writes with his finger; stone represents harsh inflexible reality in the Gospel as well as in Camus's story.

Few of Camus's works use stone more obsessively than *The Adulterous Woman*. Among many references, the most memorable is the sentence where Janine becomes aware of how the desert has disappointed her expectations of it (and we have seen how this disappointment is echoed in many other aspects of her consciousness): "Now she saw that the desert was not that at all, but merely stone, stone everywhere, in the sky full of nothing but stone-dust, rasping and cold, as on the ground, where nothing grew among the stones except dry grasses" (10).[38]

Janine's glum preoccupation with the stony desert constitutes a form of self-punishment, similar to the fear of lapidation that weighed upon the biblical adulteress. Camus has pressed the analogy further still. As the story opens, with Janine on the bus, she begins to observe her surroundings, and notices what Camus terms "the gritty fog" (4),[39] the cloud of dust and sand through which they are driving. Janine perceives this fog as a willful, hostile force: "The sand now struck the windows in packets as if hurled by invisible hands" (4).[40] Shortly afterward, when the bus has to stop, she is actually struck in the face by the grains of sand. This is not to suggest that Janine is guilty, especially of adultery, and even less that she deserves to be stoned, but rather that the biblical story informs this one, in Janine's mind as well as our own. The stoning of the bus by invisible accusers awakens her conscience. In some obscure way, she feels guilty; spurred by that anxiety, she achieves a new self-awareness.

The biblical story tells of a kind of trial, and as we have noted, the principle of law would have appealed to Camus. Camus's story does not, however, present many elements of a trial. Although one can readily see the symbolic adultery in the climactic visit to the fort, who accuses Janine? who judges her? what law condemns her? and who would punish her? Perhaps one answer, suggested in the preceding paragraph, is that the entire process occurs within Janine's mind: she accuses, judges, and ultimately forgives herself, replacing an old law of dependence and fear with a new law of independence and confidence. If so, the reader has been drawn into the procedure, and Camus has brought off an ironic reversal in the verdict, similar to Jesus'. For we readers and critics are Janine's accusers and would-be judges; we are the scribes and the Pharisees.

Peter Cryle concludes his chapter on *The Adulterous Woman* by examining "the comments of critics who *wanted to judge* the heroine's action in the light of the ideas expressed by Camus in other works." His summation is stunning: "For various reasons, they all find that Janine is guilty."[41] I find it hard to believe that Camus wrote this story so that readers could overturn Jesus' verdict on appeal. To be sure, the title invites a judgment, and Janine probably finds herself guilty. But here guilt is not the point, except as a condition for reprieve. Should we not suppose that Janine returns from the fort with a conscience instructed to go forth and sin no more? The New Testament adulteress, for all we know, may have lapsed into sin again, despite Jesus' teaching; Janine may once again sink into parasitic passivity or pine once again for an impossible freedom. The revelation of the truth is nonetheless the significant moment of the story. The adulteress goes away with at least the hope of salvation; Janine lives on with at least the hope of entering her kingdom. The lesson for the rest of us is that we should all look within ourselves and judge our own lives.

Part of Camus's genius as a writer is revealed in his choice of a subject like Janine, an unremarkable person in every respect, whose passivity and detachment have seemed to other critics the very negation of Camus's moral philosophy. The transformation of Janine's menopausal depression into an existential epiphany constitutes a literary tour de force. To be consistent with his own moral position, moreover, the author must acknowledge his solidarity with the heroine; he too must avoid passing judgment. Camus's narrative strategy in *The Adulterous Woman* sets a pattern for most of the stories that follow. In the beginning, and for the major part of the story, the reader sees through the eyes of Janine and conceptualizes through her mind. Although, as we have seen, Janine may not be a completely reliable observer, Camus does not exploit the ironic possibilities very much. In *The Adulterous Woman*, he appears to be striving for a simple and straightforward feeling of identification between reader and character. By the time of Janine's night visit to the fort, the reader should be fully involved with her.

The ending is therefore an abrupt break with the rest of the story. The narrator abandons his privilege of insight into Janine's consciousness, and gives us only a few external clues to her state of mind after the experience. We see and hear just what Marcel sees and hears: "he looked at her, without understanding" (33).[42] Most of the final paragraph, in fact, relates Marcel's actions, and mostly in plain language, except for the "light, which slapped her right in the face" (33),[43] a reminder of the sand that struck her face on the bus. Her last line—"It's nothing, dear, it's nothing" (33)[44]—has been read either as a moan of despair occasioned by her return to normality, or as an expression of protective tenderness signifying a hopeful reconciliation of her dreams and reality. Such ambiguous endings are typical of these stories; the reader is not meant to feel certain about the future projected by the story.

The story gives us an illusion of solidarity with the heroine; the real problem of the ending is whether we will be able to sustain the feeling of solidarity when we have lost the artificial support of the narrator's vision. For the reader, the problem is a reflection of Janine's own problem: can she sustain the vision of her night on the parapet? Obviously for both reader and heroine the seductive vision may turn out to be a mirage that dissipates as soon as the atmosphere changes. Janine's problem is, to be sure, a figment of the critical imagination; she has no future beyond her last words. The reader's problem, on the other hand, is real, as is also the author's. Camus wrote intending the reader's experience to be transforming. Whether or not we conclude that Janine probably will (would) find her "kingdom" or go on living in "exile," in order for her experience to affect ours, it must in some form show us how that can occur. Janine may be a person who never consciously deciphered the hiero-glyphic text of reality, or one who read the text but failed to incorporate its message in her own life. But in the metatext Camus has provided us, there is a guide to a better reading, so that we may incorporate its message in our lives.

The moment of revelation for Janine requires isolation and deprivation. This setting seems to express Camus's vision of the true nature of reality, and the Algerian desert becomes almost allegorical as the mirror of humanity's existential aloneness in a barren, meaningless creation. The warm beaches and the shut-tered apartment have deluded Janine about the world; but if the reality is less comfortable, it possesses its own beauty and its own glory, to which Janine, like the other heroes of these stories, suddenly awakens. In most cases, moreover, the awakening is solitary. How and why it happens, even what it is, have little importance, but it is crucial whether the newly enlightened person can communicate the vision to others.

Throughout his works, Camus portrays the anguish of trying to express one's vision. Joseph Grand, the improbable self-effacing hero of *The Plague*, most clearly illustrates the martyrdom of the artist; in *Exile and the Kingdom*, Jonas, Daru, the tongueless Renegade, and obviously The Silent Men all embody aspects of the failures of language and the tempta-tions of silence. So do Janine and Marcel, who have never learned the language of the Arabs all around them, and who, in the final paragraph, speak to each other without being understood. The story ends suspended between conflicting impulses. "She was weeping copiously, unable to restrain herself" (33),[45] notes the author; is she mourning a failure, or is it that the self-restraint of a lifetime has been breached? Will Janine's feelings overwhelm her reticence and establish real communication between her and Marcel, between her and others, perhaps for the first time? On the other hand, when Janine says, "It's nothing," is that a return to self-denial, or is it the ironic prelude to the disclosure of the truth, like her earlier negative mediation, "No, she was not alone . . ." (6)?[46] We cannot know; we can only share her anxiety before the effort.

It is an anxiety Camus knew well. Many critics have suggested that the painter Jonas is a gently caricatured self-portrait, that his long sterility before the white canvas parallels Camus's hesitations before the white page, and that his eventual work, a single word that could be either "solitary" or "solidary," again represents the self-contradictory impulses and ambiguous results of Camus's own writings. In a most interesting article, Brian Fitch has proposed the desert as yet another analog to the white page and the white canvas.[47] The world lies spread before the writer, with that strange "writing" to be decoded; the temptation to succumb to the cold, to weariness, to despair, is always present. Janine may have exhausted her capacity for heroism in her brief dash to the parapet; having deciphered the message for herself, she may be incapable of translating it for Marcel. The author, however, has taken up the burden in her place, and like D'Arrast bearing the stone to the Cook's hut in the final story, Camus has brought Janine's message to us. The purpose, evidently, is not that we should lose ourselves in her humdrum existence, but that her moment of triumph should enter into ours.

Given the world as it is, the materials of the artist must inevitably be the rough and uninspiring stuff of life: solitude, silence, deprivation, despair, and death. On this bleak surface, humanity must inscribe its meaning, and the artist must create the work. *The Adulterous Woman* is a work in which the least likely of subjects plays the heroic role. If self-understanding could come to Janine, one might say, it could come to anyone; Janine represents that much hope in the world. No matter that her inarticulateness dooms her revelation to go unreported, or that the dull ears of Marcel are doomed to misapprehend it; Camus is there to relieve them of the duty. The artist may be privileged in his gift of understanding, but the artist's work is the same as everyone's; Camus's task is to write Janine's dilemma for us. Author and character are partners, solidary with each other. The completed work of art, even if it portrays a failure, represents a victory for humanity; as it extends those bonds of solidarity to the reader, it can inspire only hope.

1. P. 1573: "le ciel entier s'étendait au-dessus d'elle, renversée sur la terre froide."

2. P. 1573: "il la regarda, sans comprendre. Elle pleurait, de toutes ses larmes, sans pouvoir se retenir. 'Ce n'est rien, mon chéri,' disait-elle, 'ce n'est rien.'"

3. Cryle discusses structure in his chapter on *The Adulterous Woman*, pp. 45–68. Inevitably, I repeat some of the details he cites, especially regarding the treatment of time. We reach rather different conclusions, however, and I consider more elements than he does and assign them different relative importance.

4. P. 1558: "le car était parti à l'aube"; "depuis deux heures, dans le matin froid, il progressait"; "il lui semblait qu'elle voyageait depuis des jours."

5. P. 1558: "Y avait-il si longtemps de cela? Vingt-cinq ans. Vingt-cinq ans n'étaient rien puisqu'il lui semblait que c'était hier. . . ."

6. P. 1558: "Ils avaient navigué en silence dans une sort de nuit blanche." Note that the French term "nuit blanche," literally "white night," strengthens the resemblance.

7. P. 1560: "Les années avaient passé, dans la pénombre qu'ils entretenaient, volets mi-clos. L'été, les plages, les promenades, le ciel même étaient loin."

8. P. 1559: "Non, rien ne se passait comme elle l'avait cru."

9. P. 1560: "la chaleur, les essaims de mouches, les hôtels crasseux . . . palmiers . . . sable doux."

10. P. 1557: "Insolite. . . ."

11. P. 1572: "Elle tournait avec eux [les feux] et le même cheminement immobile la réunissait peu à peu à son être le plus profond."

12. P. 1558: "un peu petit."

13. P. 1558: "où son mari et elle tenaient à peine."

14. P. 1564: "elle aurait voulu tenir moins de place."

15. P. 1569: "elle se sentait trop grande, trop épaisse."

16. P. 1572: "d'énormes burnous."

17. P. 1572: "le poids des êtres." O'Brien gives "the dead weight of others"; see my comment in the Appendix.

18. P. 1558: "première en gymnastique, son souffle était inépuisable."

19. P. 1557: "Il faisait froid."

20. P. 1560: "Elle n'avait pas pensé au froid, au vent coupant, à ces plateaux quasi polaires."

21. P. 1562: "et elle aurait voulu aller vers eux. Mais bien qu'il fût près de midi, le froid était vif; le vent la fit frissonner."

22. P. 1572: "Elle respirait, elle oubliait le froid."

23. P. 1564: "lui donnaient aussi de l'embarras."

24. P. 1572: "l'air froid qu'elle avalait par saccades coula bientot régulièrement en elle, une chaleur timide commença de naître au milieu des frissons."

25. P. 1559: "Pourtant, elle n'était pas si grosse, grande et pleine plutôt, charnelle, et encore désirable—elle le sentait bien sous le regard des hommes."

26. P. 1559: "regardait toujours devant lui."

27. P. 1562: "fixait la route, droit devant lui."

28. P. 1562: "vit d'abord le soldat qui avancait à sa rencontre. Elle attendait son sourire ou son salut. Il la dépassa sans la regarder, et disparut."

29. P. 1566: "n'avait jamais vu autant d'hommes. Pourtant, aucun ne la regardait."

30. P. 1570: "Ils s'aimaient dans la nuit, sans se voir, à tâtons. Y a-t-il un autre amour que celui des ténèbres, un amour qui crierait en plein jour? Elle ne savait pas, mais elle savait que Marcel avait besoin d'elle et qu'elle avait besoin de ce besoin, qu'elle en vivait la nuit et le jour, la nuit surtout, chaque nuit, où il ne voulait pas être seul, ni vieillir, ni mourir, avec cet air buté qu'il prenait et qu'elle reconnaissait parfois sur d'autres visages d'hommes, le seul air commun de ces fous qui se camouflent sous des airs de raison, jusqu'à ce que le délire les prenne et les jette désespérément vers un corps de femme pour y enfouir, sans désir, ce que la solitude et le nuit leur montrent d'effrayant."

31. P. 1569: "Marcel vint la rejoindre, et éteignit aussitôt sans rien lui demander."

32. See Cryle, pp. 55–58.

33. Quoted by Cryle, p. 52n: "un récit humoristique, à commencer par le titre lui-même."

34. The French text is: "Alors les scribes et les pharisiens amènent une femme surprise en adultère; et, la plaçant au milieu du peuple, ils disent à Jésus: Maître, cette femme a été surprise en flagrant délit d'adultère. Moïse, dans la loi, nous a ordonné de lapider de telles femmes: toi donc, que dis-tu? Ils disaient cela pour l'éprouver, afin de pouvoir l'accuser. Mais Jésus, s'étant baissé, écrivait avec le doigt sur la terre. Comme ils continuaient à l'interroger, il se releva et leur dit: Que celui de vous qui est sans péché jette le premier la pierre contre elle. Et s'étant de nouveau baissé, il écrivait sur la terre. Quand ils entendirent cela, accusés par leur conscience, ils se retirèrent un à un, depuis les plus âgés jusqu'aux derniers; et Jésus resta seul avec la femme qui était là au milieu. Alors s'étant relevé, et ne voyant plus que la femme, Jésus lui dit: Femme, où sont ceux qui t'accusaient? Personne ne t'a-t-il condamnée? Elle répondit: Non, Seigneur. Et Jésus lui dit: Je ne te condamne pas non plus; va, et ne pèche plus."

35. P. 1567: "Tout autour, un troupeau de dromadaires immobiles, minuscules à cette distance, formaient sur le sol gris les signes sombres d'une étrange écriture dont il fallait déchiffrer le sens."

36. Besides the biblical allusion, this scene seems to be a quotation of Dostoevski, as Stirling Haig pointed out in "The Epilog of *Crime and Punishment* and Camus's 'La

Femme adultère.'" Like Janine, Raskolnikov looks out over the Siberian landscape, hears the distant sounds, sees the nomads on the horizon, and envisions another kind of life, lived in freedom. This reinforces the association with judgment.

37. P. 1566: "On n'y rencontrait pas une seule femme et il semblait à Janine qu'elle n'avait jamais vu autant d'hommes.

38. P. 1560: "Elle voyait à présent que le désert n'était pas cela, mais seulement la pierre, la pierre partout, dans le ciel où régnait encore, crissante et froide, la seule poussière de pierre, comme sur le sol où poussaient seulement, entre les pierres, des graminées sèches."

39. P. 1557: "la brume minérale."

40. P. 1557: "Sur les vitres, le sable s'abattait maintenant par poignées comme s'il était lancé par des mains invisibles."

41. P. 66: "les commentaires des critiques qui ont voulu juger l'action de l'héroïne à la lumière des idées exprimées par Camus dans d'autres ouvrages. Pour des raisons diverses, ils trouvent tous que Janine est coupable." My italics in the English.

42. P. 1573: "il la regarda, sans comprendre."

43. P. 1573: "lumière, qui la gifla en plein visage." O'Brien gives "blinded her"; see my comment in the Appendix.

44. P. 1573: "'Ce n'est rien, mon chéri, ce n'est rien.'"

45. P. 1573: "Elle pleurait, de toutes ses larmes, sans pouvoir se retenir."

46. P. 1559: "Non, elle n'était pas seule . . ." Ellipsis in the text.

47. See Brian T. Fitch, "Camus's Desert Hieroglyphics."

 Three

The Renegade:
A Reified Voice

The Renegade, or a Confused Mind[1] has enjoyed high levels of
attention from critics, although it appears less often than some
other stories in anthologies. It is, in certain respects, the least
accessible of the six stories. By comparison with the demented
slave who is the work's hero and central consciousness, the main
characters of all the others seem like normal workaday folks.
Moreover, they go about relatively familar business for the most
part, in settings that are exotic but memorable chiefly for a kind
of blankness; certainly we find nothing to compare with the
Renegade's chosen task of assassinating the new missionary, or
with Taghâsa, the city of salt. This alienating strangeness
persists in Camus's narration as well. The dominant mode of
Exile and the Kingdom is a limited third-person viewpoint,
sustained at, or very close to, the level of the character's own
consciousness, which is itself rational and coherent. *The Artist
at Work* also breaks from this pattern, but the narrator then
exploits his superior rationality for its ironic effect. In *The
Renegade*, we hear the inner monolog—or schizoid dialog—of a
man who has completely lost touch with reason, in our familiar
sense of the term. All these factors combine to place *The
Renegade* in a modernist tradition; it reminds us of Beckett,
Kafka, or Conrad, whereas the others seem naturalistic, aspiring
to a perfect transparency of style.

   Nonetheless, the story itself is not hard to follow. The
Renegade is a former Catholic missionary who rashly undertook

to convert the city of Taghâsa, an eerie desert fortress inhabited by a notoriously cruel people. Instead of converting the Taghâsans, the Renegade is enslaved, tortured, mutilated, and ultimately converted himself to worship of a fetish. One day he overhears the news that a new missionary is to arrive, supported by French soldiers and accepted by the Taghâsans. The Renegade steals a gun, escapes, and waits in ambush to murder the new missionary. All the foregoing is, in fact, remembered by the Renegade as he waits, for a day and a night, until he finally kills the missionary. His recollections are interspersed with reactions to his present situation—the growing heat, his impatience, for example—and with thoughts about his motives and his view of the world.

The reader's response to the narrator poses the most urgent problem of interpretation in *The Renegade*. The first lines announce both the first-person perspective, rigorously maintained until the next-to-last line, and the high degree of unreliability. The subtitle, indeed, had forewarned of the central figure's confusion. His language constantly reemphasizes his incoherence: he repeats as a kind of refrain the opening words, "What a jumble," and occasionally interjects the nonsense syllables "gra gra." The syntax relies heavily on parataxis, repetition, lists of nouns without verbs, and the suppression of conjunctions. From time to time, the discourse veers abruptly, addressing a question or command to the Renegade rather than to the phantom listener, to whom most of the story seems to be an apostrophe. In rare cases, even some of the punctuation is deleted. One sentence will suffice to illustrate most of these traits: "This long, this long dream, I'm awaking, no, I'm going to die, dawn is breaking, the first light, daylight for the living, and for me the inexorable sun, the flies" (60).[2]

The Renegade's speech is undermined still more by some of what he tells of himself. He does not contradict himself, despite some inconsistency in his attitude, nor does he claim anything that violates our own sense of the possible—there are no outbreaks of the supernatural, for example. The Renegade's life, however, reveals a recurrent blindness, especially to his own motives and capacities. His religious vocation is tainted by his desire to escape his home, especially his father, about whom he mutters at one point, "one really ought to kill one's father" (36);[3] his self-abasement as a seminarian is motivated by his wish to set an example, "to be noticed" (37);[4] his mission to Taghâsa is obviously prompted by a lust for power: "I dreamed of absolute power" (39).[5] These incidents belong to a well-known tradition of self-delusion or hypocrisy; the Renegade's confusion is such that he exposes his base motives more fully than most, certainly more than necessary for the perceptive reader to form suspicions about his trustworthiness. Not only has he misapprehended his own motives, moreover, but also he has frequently failed to carry out his plan, through failure of will. He is a renegade many times over: a priest who has renounced his God, a puritan who has attempted rape, a would-be conqueror who has accepted slavery. He has no more control of his behavior than knowledge of his motives. His final action, as we eventually learn, was to be another mission. The form it takes—murder—would suffice to warn us against believing him too readily; following on what we learn of his career, his final day seems equally solipsistic. The Renegade has always confused the demands of his own ego with the external world. He is cut off from the world because he is imprisoned within his own self.

In some modernist fiction, that seems to be the point; the self is an absolute limit that cannot be transcended. The Renegade is not so mad as he first appears, however; in fact, his very awareness of his confusion distances him from it and secures a small area of agreement between him and the reader. For all its linguistic signs of irrationality, furthermore, the story unfolds with considerable structural coherence and even clarity. Peter Cryle has outlined in detail how the narration marks the time of day throughout a twenty-four hour period, dawn to dawn, and how the Renegade's life parallels this day spiritually as well as chronologically.[6] The events make a sequence and a sense, including the climactic murder.

In short, the Renegade is unreliable in his judgments, but apparently not in his facts. His judgments, moreover, concern primarily himself and his relationship to a god. He speculates infrequently about the motives of others, and completely ignores their advice. Brute, physical force alone influences his beliefs about the ultimate meaning of the universe. Protracted subjection to pain and confinement within the city of salt have changed him from a believer in the God of mercy to a believer in a god of evil. And yet, as there are hints throughout and as it is clear at the end, he has never fully lost faith in the God of mercy. His insanity results far less from the psychological trauma than from his inability to reconcile his beliefs with each other or with reality. The kingdoms he tries to found—absolute monarchies every one—are doomed to fail in doubt. Hardly has the missionary been shot when the Renegade begins to worry that Christian soldiers will govern Taghâsa after all.

It should be clear that *The Renegade* is in no sense a plausible psychological portrait, whether of a madman or some other type. Camus deliberately severed the bonds of plausibility that might have linked his text to a real interior monolog. *The Renegade* portrays rather a moral and intellectual dilemma, and the Renegade is a metaphor of the text for a particular response to that dilemma.

Obviously, religious obsession defines the Renegade more than any other quality. Each of his many denials has occurred in the name of a faith: two apostasies—he leaves his Protestant village for a Catholic seminary, he renounces the Christian God to worship the Fetish; and two betrayals—he disobeys his superiors, robs the convent, and flees to convert Taghâsa; he disobeys the Sorcerer-priest, steals the gun, and flees to hasten the coming of the kingdom of evil by killing the missionary. From his youth, he translates the natural and physical world into religious imagery: "Catholicism is the sun" (35),[7] "truth is square, heavy, thick" (54).[8] One widely held interpretation of the story treats the Renegade primarily as a symbol, abstracted almost to allegory, of the Believer, the Man of Faith. His unreliability, his solitude, his destructiveness, and his failure to establish any kingdom on earth, all these mark him as a zealot and thus as an enemy of humanity, in Camus's view. One can without difficulty extend the notion of belief to take in much more than the organized religions; any form of absolutism, political and moral as well as religious, manifests the same dehumanizing tendencies.

Camus explicitly associates the power motive to the Renegade's ostensible religious faith. His arrival at the seminary was like a Napoleonic victory for the Church—"they greeted me like the sun at Austerlitz" (36)[9]—and the Renegade never ceases equating faith and power. The appeal of Taghâsa lies in its challenge; before he went, the Renegade dreamed of his triumph: ".... I'd get the upper hand of those savages, like a strong sun"—still Austerlitz—"Strong, yes, that was the word I constantly had on the tip of my tongue, I dreamed of absolute power, the kind that makes people kneel down, that forces the adversary to capitulate, converts him in short ...." (39).[10] Of course, it is the Taghâsans, whose sun subjugates the missionary, who vanquish him, "thrown on my knees in the hollow of that white shield" (44),[11] who tear out the tongue on which he tasted the fantasy of power. And it is precisely that power he now worships in his lords and in the Fetish, about which his first thought in the moment of conversion was, "Hail, he was strength and power" (53).[12] Even as the slave of the Taghâsans, the Renegade cherishes his dream of power, and his deadly mission is undertaken for power: "O Fetish, my god over yonder, may your power be preserved" (58),[13] prays the Renegade as he loads the gun and takes aim; and when the victim falls, he says, "he is raising his head a little, he sees me—me his all-powerful shackled master" (59).[14] The Renegade spiritually accepted his own slavery because he thought it allied him with the strongest god and the strongest people.

It is easy enough to castigate the Renegade as a villain, but in Camus's world, fanatical believers, self-righteous judges, all the powerful, must be human, too. No humanism that excludes some humans, on whatever grounds, can claim to be any more than another faith, temporarily masking its absolutist imperative with a verbal screen of charity. The Renegade, after all, suffers excruciatingly for his errors, and almost any other rhetoric besides his religious self-justification would have made him seem more a sympathetic victim than a symbolic villain.

Even within the context of religious imagery, Camus has given the Renegade some affinities with figures other than the absolute Believer.

On the one hand, the Renegade appears in the beginning almost as an Everyman figure, as suffering humanity awaiting the savior. In the beginning of his monolog, the Renegade thinks of killing the missionary as a symbolic act; the missionary stands for a tradition that had failed him. Most immediately, the missionary takes the place of the Renegade's father, "my coarse father . . . my pig of a father" (35–36),[15] whose drunkenness was responsible for the son's poor health: "because of the alcohol, they have drunk sour wine and their children have decayed teeth, gra, gra, one really ought to kill one's father" (36).[16] Since the father has already drunk himself to death, "there's nothing left but to kill the missionary" (36),[17] whose title is appropriately "Father"; but even the father is just the representative of a whole society: "I have something to settle with him and with his teachers, with my teachers who deceived me, with the whole of lousy Europe, everybody deceived me" (36).[18] In a similar fashion, describing his conversion to the Fetish, he groups all his past: "down with Europe, reason, honor, and the cross" (54).[19] The tragic irony of his condition is that the long experience of slavery and pain has so filled him with hate that the object of his hatred, the symbol of his disgust, is also his savior. As in many great religious myths, notably the story of Christ, people fail to recognize the savior when he comes and kill him; and it is only this consented sacrifice that brings understanding and conversion—as perhaps it does to the Renegade, in the last paragraph.

The Renegade is thus not a simple villain but a symbol of all humanity, evil but comprehensible in his worst excesses of violence. More than that, he is not only villain but victim. His death is perhaps not certain at the end, but very probable. He says as he awakens, "I'm going to die" (60);[20] and to all appearances, he has been beaten and abandoned helpless in the desert. The figure he sees, or fancies he sees, coming to him only brutalizes him further. Moreover, the Renegade has foreseen and accepted his punishment; as the Taghâsans rush upon him after the murder, he spurs them on: "Ah, yes, strike . . . strike! strike me first . . . strike the belly, yes, strike the eyes" (59).[21] It does not, I think, vitiate his function as sacrificial scapegoat that he has throughout his life sought "to be offended," by the thinly dressed girls of Grenoble as by the cruel lords of Taghâsa. His masochistic quest for martyrdom is theologically wrong, and his death will not edify the Taghâsans. He dies, rather, for us, the readers. His very weakness, the renewed impulse to recant again, unknowable (like his life and death) outside the literary text, provides the redemptive significance to the event.

Without pride, indeed almost unconsciously, the Renegade has compared himself to Jesus. Recalling his feelings after his mutilation, and mingling them with his hatred as he waits for the missionary, he says, "he, the Lord of kindness, whose very name revolts me, I disown him, for I know him now. He dreamed and wanted to lie, his tongue was cut out so that his word would no longer be able to deceive the world, he was pierced with nails even in his head, his poor head, like mine now" (54).[22] But it was, or course, the Renegade, not Jesus, who dreamed of bringing the word and had his tongue cut out. In the final scenes, the Renegade welcomes his masters' cruelty, saying "I love the blow that nails me down crucified" (60).[23] The next morning, his delirious thoughts echo the last words of Jesus: "O Fetish, why hast thou forsaken me? All is over, I'm thirsty" (60).[24]

The allusions are unambiguous, and cannot be dismissed as part of the Renegade's self-deception. The Renegade seems unaware of the comparison, and the author must therefore have suggested it for the reader. Unless Camus intended to discredit Jesus (and the parallels are not numerous enough, forceful enough, or close enough to support that analysis), he must have meant for the image of Jesus to infuse an element of goodness into the otherwise sordid life of the Renegade. Camus's Jesus is only human, however; neither God nor Fetish answers the dying Believer's anguished cry. What is perhaps most admirable in Jesus, from the humanist's perspective, is precisely his doubt before death. The Renegade's crime, in the same perspective, is not his betrayals of his faiths but his flights to other faiths, his failure to abandon absolute faith altogether in favor of life and compromise.

The moment when the Renegade converts fully to worship of the Fetish is highly charged and merits close scrutiny. It follows immediately his most severe punishment, the mutilation. He brought that upon himself by daring to approach a woman, who had been left alone with him in the den of the Fetish. This act of desire has several rather obvious functions. In its contrast to his puritanical hostility to the girls of Grenoble, it marks the depth of his apostasy. At the same time, the horrible penalty confirms the view he has always held, that happiness, pleasure, human contacts, including sex, are evil; in this sense, the Taghâsan priest enforces the same code as the superior of his seminary. The Renegade's lust for the woman also belongs in the series of his vain efforts to usurp power and dominate; she belongs to the Sorcerer-priest and to the Fetish, and the Renegade has been disciplined not even to look during the priest's ritual copulations.

This woman is different, however, and the Renegade recalls the event as a trap deliberately set for him. The Sorcerer wears no mask for once, perhaps tempting the Renegade to see him as an equal; in any case, the Sorcerer soon leaves the Renegade alone with the woman. Her appearance is extraordinary: ". . . a new woman followed him and her face, covered with a tattoo reproducing the mask of the Fetish, expressed only an idol's ugly stupor" (52).[25] The Renegade confuses her with the Fetish, at the same time he is drawn to her body: ". . . the Fetish looked at me over that motionless body whose muscles stirred gently and the woman's idol face didn't change when I approached. Only her eyes enlarged as she stared at me, my feet touched hers, the heat then began to shriek, and the idol, without a word, still staring at me with her dilated eyes, gradually slipped onto her back, slowly drew her legs up and raised them as she gently spread her knees" (52).[26] The woman's resemblance to a god ought to have warned the Renegade that he was about to commit a sacrilege; instead, it draws him to her. He lusts for union with the god far more than he lusts for sexual gratification. What appears to be the Renegade's only gesture toward any human contact turns out to be the boldest, or most desperate, of his efforts to unite with god. Punished in so exemplary a fashion that he reminds us of those mythic Greek figures in whom Camus saw the image of humanity, the Renegade does not, however, revolt, but takes the final leap of religious faith.

Recovering in pain from his mutilation, the Renegade converts to his new god: "For the first time, as a result of offenses, my whole body crying out a single pain, I surrendered to him and approved his maleficent order" (53).[27] The Renegade has not yet found humility, however. Rallying to the forces of evil, he thinks at last that he has achieved the union he so desired. "Yes, I was to be converted to the religion of my masters, yes indeed, I was a slave, but if I too am wicked then I am no longer a slave despite my shackled feet and my mute mouth" (54).[28] The Renegade's rationalization may recall Caligula's logic. It explains in Camus's terms much of the human evil in the world. The Renegade is an extreme case, absolutely weak and subject to the absolutely cruel, but his pathetic illusion of solidarity with his god can be found everywhere. Worship, however, is not solidarity. If the Renegade ever glimpses the truth about his religion, it is only at the very end, when he at last realizes that all gods have abandoned him, for he was always alone.

In a brilliant analysis of the story, Victor Brombert writes, "The allegorical identity of the Renegade thus emerges. He is the modern intellectual" who denies "life in favor of abstraction," and who "believes he is out to convert the barbarians; in fact he seeks tyranny in order to submit to it."[29] One can scarcely deny that aspect of his makeup, but he is also more; we must not reduce the story to a parable about intellectuals, with the Renegade as exemplary villain. Still less can we accept Lawrence Joiner's vehement denunciation: "He is unsuitable for any society, unacceptable in any fraternity of man, exiled from all kingdoms, even that of evil, and fit only to be stuffed with salt."[30] It is true that the story ends with a handful of salt being stuffed into the Renegade's mouth, but the fitness of that savagery is precisely the unanswerable question. Of the various allegorical identities we have proposed, Intellectual, Zealot, Everyman, Scapegoat, which are punished fittingly? In a world constructed entirely by the Renegade's own vision, how do we receive that single apparently objective statement, that verdict of guilty and sentence of death?

Brombert observes that the murder of the missionary is a suicide. We have already seen that the Renegade's anger is directed against his father and his fatherland, for which the missionary becomes the surrogate or symbol. He comes to Taghâsa not merely as a representative of the Renegade's "cultural heritage" and "spiritual guild," in Brombert's phrase, but more importantly as a double of the Renegade. He comes as the Renegade once dreamed of coming; he is an image of the younger self, the self that might have been. The murderous shots and the sadistic bludgeoning to finish the killing express self-loathing and self-destruction in an extreme degree. The "wrenching" of which Cryle speaks[31] is given physical form. The Renegade not only remembers how he has changed, not only still believes without following; he must also confront the unchanged, still obedient self in the person of the missionary. The Renegade has never believed in reconciliations; the only cure he knows is conquest of one by the other. Therefore he kills his despised former self.[32]

The missionary is not the only double, however; in fact, the Renegade's whole inner monolog is a phantasmagoria of self-projections. The Sorcerer-priest, first of all, realizes the very ambition the Renegade had cherished. The Sorcerer possesses power, the Sorcerer looks and does not turn his gaze away, the Sorcerer converts the missionary. Although the Renegade does not himself understand it, to the reader this ironic reversal exposes the Renegade's real motives: lust for power. The Sorcerer, and indeed the Taghâsans of whom he is the spiritual representative, embody the Renegade's unavowed ideals. We have seen how this will to dominate survives even his torture and enslavement; to the end, he dreams of union with the ultimate symbol of power and cruelty, the Fetish itself.

On the other hand, the woman whom the Sorcerer violates before the Fetish reflects a repressed animal self. The first time, when the Renegade watches, he stresses the animal-like elements in the scene, the woman "on all fours" (49),[33] all the faces hidden by masks, by clothes, by turning to the wall, the priest, the woman, and finally the Renegade howling to the Fetish—after which he is kicked up against the wall like an annoying dog. From then on, he feels desire as he hears the daily cries of the woman and sees "the bestial shadows moving on the wall" (50).[34] Finally the Sorcerer leaves the tattooed woman alone, and the Renegade succumbs to the desire for her body—"the only thing alive about her was her thin flat body" (52)[35]—only to be torn from her and punished by having his tongue cut off—"was it I screaming with that bestial scream" (52)[36]—and by being beaten "on the sinful place" (52).[37] As with the other selves, the Renegade cannot integrate his sexuality. In Grenoble, he conquered it; in Taghâsa, it conquers him, until his masters by crude force destroy it.

In the final paragraph, the figure who appears to the dying Renegade represents yet another double, the merciful savior. However little he understood it himself, the Renegade's mission included the task of preaching love and forgiveness. Consequently, he sees in this figure a possibility of return to the beginning: "we'll begin all over again, we'll rebuild the city of mercy, I want to go back home. Yes, help me, that's right, give me your hand . . ." (61).[38] This pathetic and doomed appeal is, however, apparently addressed to the Sorcerer, the Renegade's master; and so this last double combines elements of all aspects of the Renegade's confused spirit, even the sensual, for he has suddenly become "my beloved master" (61).[39] Moreover, like the women, the Sorcerer has now become a victim, vanquished by the soldiers—or perhaps even punished by his own people, for he seems to have been mutilated like the Renegade: "Here, here, who are you, torn, with bleeding mouth, it is you, Sorcerer . . ." (61).[40] The Renegade had imagined Jesus, too, with his tongue cut out (55). In this last vision, then, the Renegade finally succeeds in unifying his selves within a single self, ambiguous, of course, for it is simultaneously master and victim, past and future, male and female, African and European, and all the other paradoxes of humanness.

The Renegade's tendency to divide into doubles points to his role as a scapegoat. René Girard has analyzed the mechanism by which religious ritual reenacts a society's founding violence, but in such a way as to mystify and legitimize it. The victim must be transformed into a monster, so that the expulsion or slaughter seems necessary and right. At the same time, the victim must remain a member of the society, like the survivor-judges, or else the transfer of their guilt onto the scapegoat does not take place.[41]

At the center of *The Renegade* is the primitive religion of fetish worship, with the daily sexual sacrifice of a woman and the continued sacrificial service of the enslaved and mutilated Renegade. The Taghâsans practice a cult of such barbaric cruelty that no reader can fail to perceive its origin in violence. Yet fetish worship is a double for the Renegade's Christianity, just as the Sorcerer is a double for the missionary. In the end, both men become scapegoats, mutilated and cast out. The Renegade was from the start fatally other and monstrous to the Taghâsans; the Sorcerer becomes so only as his prestige wanes. Both, at least in the Renegade's delirium, rejoin the archetypal scapegoat figure of the crucified Christ.

It is tempting for us as readers to regard the Renegade as our own scapegoat. His arrogance, intolerance, and lust for power make him monstrous to us, and we may well join in his execution by finding it justified. Yet the doubles must somewhere include the reader. If, as Girard argues, great works of literature demystify the ritual sacrifice by exposing the violent origins of the sacred, *The Renegade* belongs among them. In the final fusion of the Renegade's doubles, his ultimate self is dominated by the best virtues of liberal humanism, hope, charity, courage, mercy, love. As we condemn him, we discover that he was one of us, deserving not death but a merciful hand.

Alas, the hand held out to him was a punishing hand; his recantation in extremis, his return to love, is not to be rewarded by a providentially rigged conclusion. The world outside is indifferent to the inner world; to a soul in need of mercy and forgiveness, the world is a hostile environment. The Renegade has tasted salt before, in the hut of the Fetish, "biting the salt, as I am biting this rock today" (49),[42] and the bitterness is no doubt kin to the bitter wine he grew up on and dreamed of escaping. Such is the nourishment the world offers. At the end, of course, it is thrust upon him by another human as a judgment. But we are not meant to join in that judgment. Whatever disapproval, even hatred, we may feel for the Renegade, we cannot side with the brutal Taghâsans in executing him. Rather we should be aware of the irony in this understanding come too late. In fact, the Renegade has no language and no tongue with which to address his plea to the Sorcerer; he has doomed himself long ago to die in absolute solitude. Furthermore, it is his own double who administers the coup de grâce. Those selves he had tried to suppress, even by murder, those voices he had tried to silence, return together, but they survive only for an instant. Reunited with his dominant, negating self, they cancel one another in death.

A reading such as this, which turns the character and the story in upon itself, demonstrates a structural coherence and formal beauty that are agreeable, perhaps even instructive, to contemplate, but only skirt the question of the story's meaning. And Camus insists that writing have meaning. If the Renegade is more than just an allegorical figure of evil, specifically of the Western intellectuals' suicidal attraction to absolutism, how else can we relate so exceptional and isolated a case to our own concerns?

It is instructive, first, to replace the *Renegade* in its context in *Exile and the Kingdom.* It is the second story, following the *Adulterous Woman*; and despite the many obvious differences, there are also many surprising similarities. The setting of both is the Saharan desert, and in both, a spiritually isolated European experiences a new and overwhelming social isolation among an alien race and physical isolation in a desolate region. Both central characters are silent, both feel the decline of their bodies into painful burdens binding them to the ground, while Others appear to move effortlessly. In both stories, the narrative of a brief present time—about a day and a night—told from the perspective of this central character is paralleled by a recapitulate life. Moreover, though the Renegade's story is a first-person monolog and Janine's is a limited third-person, they share a lyricism generally absent from the other stories. This extends even to a common image, "the water of night" (33, 51),[43] symbol of an ineffably refreshing communion with nature. The themes of their thoughts are similar, too; Janine is obsessed with sexuality, with, as we have seen, latent religious implication; the Renegade reverses the emphasis, but in both cases, both themes are present and intertwined. Finally, both stories end on the same ambiguous note, with an abrupt change of narrative perspective and a punishment dealt to the central figure.

One could, therefore, propose similar readings of both stories. The central characters have misspent their lives, and the stories tell of a moment when they glimpse the truth they have missed previously. This truth, of course, lies in their own way of perceiving, rather than in any implicit cosmology. What they understand nevertheless remains incommunicable, and no uplifting transformation occurs in their lives. Only the intervention of the imaginative artist, Camus, enables us to sympathize with these remote and difficult beings.

Two important differences must be noted, however. First, in *The Renegade*, every comparable element is intensified. He goes deeper into the Desert, is more alone, is literally mute, is actually mutilated, is limited to the first person, and so forth. His revolt is not symbolic sin but a real murder. Second, the story ends with his death. Janine's future held at least the possibility of transformation, or of happiness through a transformed consciousness. For the Renegade, no hope is conceivable. His story is related from the very brink of eternal silence, and it is in this unique situation that we must look for the particular meaning of *The Renegade*.

Despite the links with the *Adulterous Woman*, *The Renegade* stands out in *Exile and the Kingdom* as strange. As we remarked at the beginning of the chapter, the characters, the setting, the technique are all exceptional. This is a story that seems to wrench away from its context.

The hero, moreover, is a character always in flight from his surroundings. He is a Catholic seminarian from a Protestant region, and he demanded to go to Taghâsa and went against orders when refused. There, as a captive, he has lived in perfect isolation. Yet, like a Chinese box, his mind has fled from its context, too. In desiring to go to Taghâsa, he recalls, "I was sure of reasoning logically on that subject, never quite sure of myself otherwise, but once I get an idea I don't let go of it, that's my strong point, yes the strong point of the fellow they all pitied!" (40).[44] Hardly has he been taken captive, however, when this "strong point" deserts him before the Fetish: "no one spoke but me, the jumble was beginning in my head" (47).[45] Since that time, a voice, detached, uncontrollable, has been speaking within his mind; on this image the story opens: "What a jumble! What a jumble! I must tidy up my mind. Since they cut out my tongue, another tongue, it seems, has been constantly wagging somewhere in my skull, something has been talking, or someone, that suddenly falls silent and then it all begins again—oh, I hear too many things I never utter, what a jumble, and if I open my mouth it's like pebbles rattling together" (34).[46]

The narrator is still another disembodied tongue. The hero's radical inability to communicate throws any purported transcription of his thoughts into high relief as an autonomous object, with no plausible context.

If, in conventional thinking, we can dovetail these levels of perception as we have just done—that is to say, the story generates a situation, which in turn generates a character, who generates thought, which generates a text—in reality only the text exists and begets all the others. *The Renegade* presents a text that declares its independence from any ostensible contexts; all the generative connections are severed. The story is simultaneously image, analysis, and example of the absurd, of a universe where no meaningful relations exist. To take cognizance of this fundamental meaninglessness, however, reveals only half of a paradox. The story may signify meaninglessness, but all the acts surrounding the story—writing, reading, criticizing—reveal at least the desire to deny, overcome, or transcend that meaninglessness. The Renegade, even though he cannot discover the order he seeks, produces a highly structured "jumble"; and Camus, although he denies his hero the solace of an answer to his quest, provides an answer for the reader.

That answer cannot be the simple discovery of an order, but rather a discovery that takes place within ourselves. It will not transform the world. All the stories stop short of depicting the hero after the moment of illumination. *The Renegade* belongs to a special type of story, like Flaubert's *A Simple Heart* and Tolstoy's *Death of Ivan Ilych*, where the novelist's privilege of omniscience takes us beyond the limits of human communication to the very edge of nonexistence. The deathbed revelation has no practical value to the dead person; it seems almost a parody here of the Christian doctrine that a repentance in the instant of death may have occurred and would suffice for God to save the sinner's soul. The Renegade does not pass over into the Hereafter.

His end nonetheless helps explain the other stories. His excesses have taken him as far as one can go away from human solidarity. He has made an ideal of exile and has tried to follow it. At the end, however, he still yearns for human contact, and from an exile beyond all possibility of communication, Camus dares to transmit that yearning. For Camus himself, this story risks being a betrayal. The hero lies outside the bounds of Camus's moral sense, and the text lies outside the bounds of credibility. Yet in risking this double breach of his principles, Camus effectively transcends a barrier to solidarity. Even this lost creature, abominable in his slavery as in his pride, denied all means of communication, even he was one of us, suffering in exile, longing to return to his kingdom. In this universal longing, Camus found the best hope, if not for order, for human happiness.

Despite its barrenness and horror, *The Renegade* is not necessarily angry or pessimistic. At the end, we are left to judge, as we were with Janine. The Renegade, whose real voice is that of the stony desert itself—"if I open my mouth it's like pebbles rattling together" (34)—has tried to make an ethical order of the indifference of nature. As he lived, so has he died; perhaps we may admire the relentless consistency of that universal principle.

Yet we need not ourselves reaffirm the sentence of death, nor should we join in the execution. Camus has shown how the human mind can construct a meaning around that creature reduced to bestiality; in the same way, we can construct a meaning around a formless universe.

1. The English edition eliminates the subtitle; see the Appendix for comments on problems of translation, which are numerous in this story.

2. P. 1591: "Ce long ce long rêve, je m'éveille, mais non, je vais mourir, l'aube se lève, la première lumière le jour pour d'autres vivants, et pour moi le soleil inexorable, les mouches."

3. P. 1578: "tuer son père, voilà ce qu'il faudrait."

4. P. 1578: "pour qu'on me voie."

5. P. 1579: "je rêvais du pouvoir absolu."

6. Cryle, pp. 69–70.

7. P. 1578. "le catholicisme c'est le soleil."

8. P. 1587: "la vérité est carrée, lourde, dense."

9. P. 1578: "ils m'ont vu arriver comme le soleil d'Austerlitz."

10. P. 1579: "je subjuguerais ces sauvages, comme un soleil puissant. Puissant, oui, c'était le mot que sans cesse, je roulais sur ma langue, je rêvais du pouvoir absolu, celui qui fait mettre genoux à terre, qui force l'adversaire à capituler, le convertit enfin. . . . ."

11. P. 1582: "jeté à genoux au creux de ce bouclier blanc."

12. P. 1587: "Salut, il était la force et la puissance."

13. P. 1590: "Ô fétiche, mon dieu là-bas, que ta puissance soit maintenue."

14. P. 1590: "il dresse un peu la tête, me voit, moi, son maître entravé tout-puissant."

15. Pp. 1577–78: "mon père grossier . . . ce porc."

16. P. 1578: "à cause de l'alcool, ils ont bu le vin aigre et leurs enfants ont des dents cariées, râ râ tuer son père, voilà ce qu'il faudrait."

17. P. 1578: "il ne reste qu'à tuer le missionnaire."

18. P. 1578: "J'ai un compte à régler avec lui et avec ses maîtres qui m'ont trompé, avec la sale Europe, tout le monde m'a trompé."

19. P. 1588: "à bas l'Europe, la raison et l'honneur et la croix."

20. P. 1591: "je vais mourir."

21. P. 1590: "ah! ah! oui, frappez . . . frappez, frappez sur moi d'abord . . . frappez au ventre, oui, frappez aux yeux."

22. P. 1588: "lui, l'autre, le Seigneur de la douceur, dont le seul nom me révulse, je le renie, car je le connais maintenant. Il rêvait et il voulait mentir, on lui a coupé la langue pour que sa parole ne vienne plus tromper le monde, on l'a percé de clous jusque dans la tête, sa pauvre tête, comme la mienne maintenant."

23. P. 1591: "j'aime ce coup qui me cloue crucifié."

24. P. 1591: "ô fétiche pourquoi m'as-tu abandonné? Tout est fini, j'ai soif."

25. P. 1586: "une nouvelle femme le suivait dont le visage, couvert d'un tatouage qui lui donnait le masque du fétiche, n'exprimait rien qu'une stupeur mauvaise d'idole."

26. Pp. 1586–87: "le fétiche me contemplait par-dessus ce corps immobile, mais dont les muscles remuaient doucement et le visage d'idole de la femme n'a pas changé quand je me suis approché. Ses yeux seuls se sont agrandis en me fixant, mes pieds touchaient les siens, la chaleur alors s'est mise à hurler, et l'idole, sans rien dire, me regardant toujours de ses yeux dilatés, s'est renversée peu à peu sur le dos, a ramené lentement ses jambes vers elle, et les a élevées en écartant doucement les genoux."

27. P. 1587: "Pour la première fois, à force d'offenses, le corps entier criant d'une seule douleur, je m'abandonnai à lui et approuvai son ordre malfaisant."

28. P. 1588: "Oui, je devais me convertir à la religion de mes maîtres, oui oui j'étais esclave, mais si moi aussi je suis méchant je ne suis plus esclave, malgré mes pieds entravés et ma bouche muette."

29. *The Intellectual Hero*, p. 230.

30. "Camus's 'Le Rénégat': Identity Denied," p. 41.

31. P. 72: "déchirement" is Cryle's term.

32. Onomasiologists will observe that the new missionary's name is Father Beffort (56). His role as surrogate for the Renegade's father has already been mentioned. His name is a complex bilingual pun; in French it once again suggests strength ("fort," "effort"), in English the return to the past ("before") and to faith ("be for").

33. P. 1585: "à quatre pattes."

34. P. 1585: "les ombres bestiales qui s'agitaient sur la paroi."

35. P. 1586: "Seul vivait son corps mince et plat."

36. P. 1587: "était-ce moi qui hurlais de ce cri de bête"

37. P. 1587: "à l'endroit du péché."

38. P. 1591: "nous recommencerons, nous referons la cité de miséricorde, je veux retourner chez moi. Oui, aide-moi, c'est cela, tends ta main, donne . . ." Ellipsis in the text.

39. P. 1591: "mon maître bien-aimé."

40. P. 1591: "Voici, voici, qui es-tu, déchiré, la bouche sanglante, c'est toi, sorcier. . . ."

41. See *La Violence et le sacré*, and "The Underground Critic" in *To Double Business Bound*", pp. 36–60.

42. P. 1585: "mordant le sel, comme je mords aujourd'hui le rocher."

43. Pp. 1573, 1586: "l'eau de la nuit."

44. P. 1580: "j'étais certain de bien raisonner là-dessus, jamais très sûr de moi autrement, mais mon idée quand je l'ai, je ne la lâche plus, c'est ma force, oui, ma force à moi dont ils avaient tous pitié!"

45. P. 1584: "personne ne parlait, que moi, la bouillie commençait déjà dans ma tête."

46. P. 1577: "Quelle bouillie, quelle bouillie! Il faut mettre de l'ordre dans ma tête. Depuis qu'ils m'ont coupé la langue, une autre langue, je ne sais pas, marche sans arrêt dans mon crâne, quelque chose parle, ou quelqu'un qui se tait soudain et puis tout recommence, ô j'entends trop de choses que je ne dis pourtant pas, quelle bouillie, et si j'ouvre la bouche, c'est comme un bruit de cailloux remués."

 Four

The Silent Men:
Muted Symbols

Of the six stories in *Exile and the Kingdom, The Silent Men* has
had the most baffled reception. The muteness of the characters
seems to have spread to the critics. Did Roger Quilliot mean to
be witty when he wrote, "There is nothing to say about *The
Silent Men*"? Nowhere else does his chapter have that flippant
character, and, to be fair, Quilliot goes on to add, "except that
one reads it straight through without stopping, that the characters impress upon us their presence, their poor happinesses,
their pride as artisans, their angers and their powerlessness."[1]
Even so, it is a meager commentary. Peter Cryle, in the chapter
he devotes to *The Silent Men*, observes that such remarks make
up virtually all the criticism of the story.[2]

It is true that not much happens. The main character, a
cooper named Yvars, returns to his job the day following the
collapse of a strike. He and his fellow workmen slowly regain
their former feelings of camaraderie for one another while
remaining resentful toward their boss, Lassalle, an affable and
well-meaning man, who makes a few maladroit efforts to be
cordial. In the afternoon, Lassalle's daughter is stricken with an
unidentified malady and falls unconscious; she is rushed to a
hospital. The men, although somewhat moved, do not offer any
words of sympathy to Lassalle. Yvars returns home in the
evening, and the story concludes with his nostalgic longing to
escape a vague feeling of depression and perhaps guilt. The
characters offer no more critical promise than does the plot;

only Yvars is developed with any thoroughness, and his chief trait is an open-minded but simple candor.

Cryle himself examines primarily the ideas—social, political, and moral—and formulates an interpretation of the ending. He notes in passing, however, that many critics, including Quilliot, have flatly denied any symbolic value to this realistic writing, to which he responds, "One must recognize that the presence of *The Silent Men* in *Exile and the Kingdom* tends perforce to link it to the other stories, all five of them rich in symbolic resonances."[3] The only example he gives, however, is the sentence: "The workshop had become too big for the handful of men who worked there" (71).[4] In view of the general deafness of readers to the symbolic resonances, it would seem worthwhile to call attention to some more of them.

Symbolic, as Cryle uses it, is a loose term, covering several types of allusive representation. Since all of them have been equally ignored in the story, the broad application of the term seems justified. Lest there be confusion, however, let me make clear that by *symbol* I do not mean an object that stands for one specific other object, or an object that relates Camus's work to an established set of such symbols, like Freudian or Christian symbolism. As I use the term *symbol*, it means the description of an object or action in such a way that it suggests meanings beyond the ordinary references of the language, especially: (1) things that embody in an external reality the internal thoughts of the character; (2) things that evoke strong associations, literary or other, in the reader's mind; (3) things that link parts of the story or different stories together intertextually through words, objects, or scenes, as opposed to linking them logically or chronologically, for example. Such uses of language are readily acknowledged in a wide range of authors, especially in the twentieth century, and even in other works by Camus; but it has commonly been assumed that Camus was striving for a more literal rendering of some external reality, especially in *The Silent Men*. Yet in the context of the other stories, the world of *The Silent Men* is rich in symbolic objects and events; their un-recognized presence is, in the end, part of the meaning of the story.

Like the other three stories told in the third person, but with a limited point of view, *The Silent Men* begins with a notation of the setting: "It was the dead of winter and yet a radiant sun was rising over the already active city. At the end of the jetty, sea and sky fused in a single dazzling light" (62).[5] Apparently straight-forward, this description already links *The Silent Men* to *The Adulterous Woman, The Guest*, and *The Growing Stone*. In the three Algerian stories, the weather is in some fashion anomalous; Janine had expected heat in the desert but finds wintry cold; Daru's school is isolated by an October snowstorm coming hard on months of summer drought; Yvars sets out on a radiant day in the middle of winter. Since all three central characters discover their "exile" during the course of the story, the incongruous weather seems to function as an early sign of their incongruous situation.

Furthermore, as each of the four stories begins, the central character is isolated from the horizon, Janine by the sandstorm, Daru by the blizzard, D'Arrast by the foggy night, and Yvars by the morning glare. One might say that they have lost their metaphorical bearings. Janine, D'Arrast, and Yvars, all traveling at the beginning, seem to be enclosed in a psychic shell, cut off not only from their fellow human beings but also from the natural world; the stories relate their breaking out of the shell, if only temporarily.

As one might expect, then, the motifs recur throughout the stories, to reflect the characters' evolution. By the time Janine goes up to the fort at night, the wind has fallen and the sky is clear. On the second day of *The Guest*, the sun comes out again, the snow melts, the path and the rocks reappear. When D'Arrast awakens on his first day in Iguape, a fine rain is falling; but on the day of the procession, the sun is out and the sky is clear. So, too, Yvars, who began with his head lowered and the dazzling light hiding the horizon (which in any case he no longer liked to look at in the morning), is seated on his terrace at the end, "the sky was becoming transparent; over the wall the soft evening sea was visible" (83).[6] Obviously, there are significant differences from story to story: Yvars has probably the most limited self-awareness of the four characters, and his confrontation with the external world seems to hold the least promise of change. Appropriately, he watches twilight fall at the end and welcomes the gentle blurring of perceptions, whereas the others have encountered the harsh light of truth.

The horizon has a particular importance in Camus's symbolic world. Janine sees the strange writing at the horizon on her first climb to the parapet, Daru and Yvars both look to the horizon at the end; moreover, in the beginning, Camus often specifically mentions that the horizon is obscured. As the place of contact between the impossible purity of the sky and the hard reality of the earth, it is the locus for a kind of truth. Yet it is inaccessible, always fugitive; the heroes who seem to have come closest to the kingdom, Jonas and D'Arrast, find it indoors. The Renegade, on the other hand, awaiting the appearance of his victim— "Nothing, still nothing from here to the horizon" (37)[7]—Daru looking at the sky, the plateau, and "beyond, the invisible lands stretching all the way to the sea" (109),[8] and Yvars, nostalgically supposing that he and Fernande were still young and "they would have gone away, across the sea" (84),[9] all seem to have failed in some significant way. But Yvars is an uncertain case. His wistfulness can scarcely pass for an active assumption of human responsibility. At the same time, Camus places him at home, looking out from the shelter of his walled terrace, in the company of his family; he does not seem exiled. For Yvars (as for Janine and for Joseph Grand in *The Plague*), the resolution may seem perilously close to mere resignation. The quality that transforms poverty and humility into human happiness, Camus seems to imply, can come only from within, through a particular form of honesty to one's self. This increasing emphasis on individual happiness rather than mass political action surely contributed to the poor reception of *The Silent Men* among French leftist critics.

In any case, it is clear that Camus has organized his natural settings so as to provide a discreet symbolic accompaniment to the psychological and philosophical movements of his stories. Paul Fortier has looked at some of the other elements in this universe, linking them to the novels as well: the sun, which signifies violence, and the sea, reconciliation, for example.[10]

Fortier treats *The Adulterous Woman, The Guest,* and *The Renegade*, in addition to the novels. One may dispute some of the precise symbolic values and prefer a less schematic analysis; nonetheless, the point stands for *The Silent Men* as well as for the other works: the natural environment is at the same time a realistic element and a symbolic matrix underlying the significant actions of the story.

Yvars himself is a fortyish man with a bad leg, who feels himself aging, especially on the morning bicycle ride to the factory. Cryle and others have noticed Yvars's striking similarity to Janine; both of them once delighted in sea bathing, but have fallen out of the habit and into poor physical condition. Cryle is wrong, it seems to me, to emphasize the differences between the two, and to argue that "the workman has none of the sluggish heaviness of the bourgeois housewife."[11] Camus writes in the third sentence, "he was cycling heavily" (62);[12] and in the third paragraph, "This morning he was pedaling along with head down, feeling even heavier than usual; his heart too was heavy" (64–65).[13] A cliché is here revitalized into a metaphor. It is true that Yvars's heaviness relates more to his stiffness than to his size; but just as Janine tries to occupy less space on her seat, Yvars has to squeeze between the tram rails and the automobiles, while his lunch bag thumps against his side, an unpleasant reminder of his situation, as Marcel's jostling is to Janine.

This is not so much to demonstrate an identity between the two as to stress the identical functions of their bodies in the two stories. Moreover, we find that same motif in other stories; Daru, although short, is "square" (89)[14] and powerful: "if need be, he could break his adversary in two" (101).[15] D'Arrast first appears with "his huge broad frame . . . planted on the ground and weighed down by fatigue" (160).[16] In every case, the size, or power, or vigor, or health, of the Europeans is contrasted to the frailty of the Arabs or Brazilians. Yet in a paradoxical correlation, the thin people seem most comfortable in the world, least exiled, as it were. The contrast is not wholly between Europeans and others, either; the French soldier on the bus with Janine is "long and thin, so thin . . . that he seemed constructed of a dry, friable material, a mixture of sand and bone" (7).[17] One could hardly express more explicitly his belonging to the desert. Monsieur Lassalle, Yvars's boss, is an example of quite a different sort; but he too is "thin and dark," and "he looked at ease in his body" (73).[18]

The body is, logically enough, the strongest link between the human mind and the external world. Since the pattern in the four third-person stories is always an abrupt realization of the central figure's situation in the world, the body serves as an early sign of the awakening consciousness, much like the weather imagery. The vague physical uneasiness of the beginning, however, leads to deeper and deeper exploration of the causes, and finally reveals an overwhelming sense of alienation. The material form of the body plays on its literal meaning and its common metaphorical meanings, from "dullness" to "importance." As with the jackal-soldier, the body's matter resembles that of the material universe; for the main characters, it stiffens.

The body is, then, almost an index to the characters' state of alienation, or awareness of it. Those who are perceived as lords or citizens of the "kingdom" appear to be weightless. That is, of course, an illusion, as is occasionally demonstrated by such characters as the Cook in *The Growing Stone* or by Lassalle with his rumpled hair and his halting gait at the end of *The Silent Men*. The nostalgia of Yvars and Janine for their lost youth includes most powerfully a longing to be free of their bodies, and to regain that illusory unconcern about their place in the physical world. Real strength and a secure place in the kingdom can come, however, only when that weight of materiality has been recognized and accepted—as D'Arrast most graphically illustrates. Janine, likewise, transcends her body's burden in her sprint to the parapet. Yvars gives less indication that he has understood and seized his responsibility; his final words appear to shift the blame to the boss, and his last thoughts are a wish for evasion. At the same time, the little girl's illness has troubled him, and she "accompanied" him on his bicycle; her memory may be the stone he is now bearing. Moreover, *The Silent Men* recounts a day that is far more ordinary than in any of the other stories; Yvars, like his co-workers, goes through a routine. One can easily project the regular recurrence of most of the day's activities, including Yvars's stiff-legged and heavy-hearted ride to the factory. The new burden of solidarity with the boss will simply be added to the heavy load he is already loyally carrying.

The turning point in *The Silent Men* occurs when the boss's daughter is stricken. As in several of the stories, Camus actually shifts the action into an entirely new course. In *The Adulterous Woman*, the title and the early part of the narrative lead the reader to expect an encounter between Janine and the French soldier; but then he disappears, and we realize that the conflict is between opposing sides of Janine herself. In *The Guest*, we begin—indeed continue right up to the end—to look for a confrontation between Daru and the prisoner, only to realize finally that the unseen "brothers" are the real adversary. In *The Silent Men*, the first half of the story seems to build toward a clash between the triumphant boss and the embittered workmen; yet in the end, the workmen, or at least Yvars, must confront their own inability to respond to the boss's suffering and the fact of the little girl's vulnerability.

Although Camus has worked one or two allusions to the girl's illness into the first pages, her story erupts brutally into the midst of the other, announced by the urgent ringing of Lassalle's bell. As Cryle and others have said, this bell represents the distance between the boss and his employees; it is a sign of the boss's muteness, of the reduction of human communication to the impersonal noise of a bell. Not all noise has negative implications, though; the hum of the saws and the regular rhythm of the hammer indicate vitality in the workshop. The ring of the bell for the girl's attack is different, however; "[The bell] was insistent, but in such a strange way, with stops and imperious starts, that the men interrupted their work" (79).[19] The urgency of the communication has to an extent humanized the offensive ringing.

This noise, which shatters their routine, seems a sign of destiny. Yvars, of course, never articulates such an idea; Camus merely implies it, by having Yvars think of death just before the bell sounds. In the other stories, too, inarticulate sounds announce the impending changes. Janine, in her bed, hears the barking of the dogs and the liquid noise of the wind, and they seem to her an irresistible appeal. Daru hears mysterious rustling noises about his schoolhouse, during the night and just as he leaves in the morning. It is as if the material universe had its own voice, to speak to those who were prepared to listen. More realistically, we can interpret these appeals as devices of point of view: the characters, already disposed to break out of old habits of thought and behavior, troubled by such factors as a disturbing environment and a cumbersome body, begin to hear messages and see codes in the natural world around them. Lassalle's bell has its full resonance only in the context of the collection. In the stories most like *The Silent Men*, there are similar sounds, signifying the imminent collapse of a familiar vision of the world.

Yvars's first thoughts as he rides to work turn on the sandwich in his lunch bag; it is a source of bitterness because it is just cheese, rather than the omelette or steak he likes. From this detail, Camus derives most of the exposition. As a realistic observation, it is a sign of the deprivations caused by the strike. Food is one of Camus's most frequent symbols, however, so that the sandwich takes on values far more extensive than mere description. In the middle of the day, as the men break for lunch, the once deprecated cheese becomes a source of pure joy for Yvars as he offers half of it to Saïd, who has none at all. Yvars is able to protect Saïd's dignity by telling him, "Then it'll be your turn to treat" (77),[20] indicating an equality that transcends their economic and racial differences. Moreover, the mere prospect of the gesture sufficed to abolish the uneasiness created by Lassalle's airs of superiority: "The uneasy feeling that hadn't left him since the interview with Lassalle suddenly disappeared to make room for a pleasant warmth" (77).[21] A few moments later, Esposito produces a jar of coffee, the gift of a grocer as a sign of sympathy with the workmen. Passing it around in a mustard jar, or drinking it straight from the pan, the men share a moment of true brotherhood.

The communal meal is one of the oldest rituals of humanity, and Camus's use of it in *The Silent Men* is not particularly unusual. There is a touching reprise at the end, when Yvars and Fernande share an aperitif. Then Yvars can at last look at his beloved sea, and can at last speak: "he told her everything" (83).[22] Eating together is a sign of communication, a communion. It is only when one places *The Silent Men* in context of the other stories, however, that Camus's stress on the symbol becomes apparent. In *The Adulterous Woman*, Janine and Marcel eat an anticommunal meal, of pork and wine. Marcel enjoys the fact that those foods are forbidden to the Arabs, but Janine feels heavier and sleepier afterward. Daru shares a meager meal with his Arab prisoner, and seems thereby to have inspired some kind of trust in him. D'Arrast accepts a glass of sweet liqueur and a meal of beans from the poor Brazilian family whose circle he is invited to join at the end, and his principal contact with the Brazilians comes through a cook; on the other hand, a drink with the notables leads to the disagreeable incident with the Police Chief, although D'Arrast is able to reestablish harmony at a later meal with them. The Renegade is forced several times to drink bitter liquids as his masters convert him to the service of a god of death; the story ends with his being given a mouthful of salt, when he was perishing of thirst.

Food and drink are therefore more than mere social rites. The nature of the food and the way it is offered and received symbolize the relationships among people and their relationships to the world—or to their gods. In *The Silent Men*, the symbolism is all positive. The sandwich, the coffee, and the anisette are simple, even poor, but wholesome. They are offered and taken in a spirit of real brotherhood. They thereby underscore some of the moments when Yvars is able to escape the pain of his situation and by human solidarity to transcend the alienation imposed by the harsh laws of economics, politics, and reality.

Like eating, washing is a social custom with a long tradition of symbolism, but Camus's use of it in *The Silent Men* is not repeated in the other stories. Its most obvious reference is to Pilate's washing his hands as he sends Jesus to the Crucifixion. The first mention in the story has barely noticeable symbolic overtones; when the boss rings for Marcou and Yvars to come to his office, "Yvars's first impulse was to go and wash his hands, but Marcou grasped him by the arm as he went by and Yvars limped out behind him" (75).[23] Yvars's reflex and Marcou's interruption seem to be symbolic only at the most superficial level, that of courtesy and of evident class distinctions. No doubt the imagery of "dirty hands" appealed to Camus, as to Sartre, in large part because of its aptitude for expressing this contrast between the worker and the clean, irresponsible bourgeois. The first meaning of the impulse is quite clearly to show deference to the boss, and Marcou stops Yvars in order to stress the barriers remaining between them. In the light of the story as a whole, however, Yvars's reaction also tells something about his character as contrasted to Marcou's; for Marcou, the union delegate, most aggressively rejects any return to cordiality, whereas Yvars often thinks of responding more warmly and on occasion even does so, as when he claps Ballester on the shoulder. The apparent contrast may, of course, be due only to our privileged insight into Yvars's thoughts; from the outside, Marcou appears hostile and rigid, but we know nothing of his private thoughts. From Lassalle's point of view, Yvars probably seems no different, but we know his feelings and can sympathize with his failure to speak and act. By the end of the story, it also seems that Marcou (or Camus) intends the unwashed hands to symbolize the workers' refusal to give up their principles. This symbolism comes very near the traditional meaning of washing. Lassalle wants to make a clean sweep of the recent past and begin afresh; Marcou and the workers are not (yet) willing to abandon what they have fought for. They will not disclaim what they have done.

As they prepare to leave, however, they do wash—except for Yvars. The previous incident is exactly reversed when Lassalle, returning from the hospital, passes through the room where the men are dressing. They all know about the little girl's attack, and can see Lassalle's grief, but say nothing. Yvars "thought that it was up to Marcou to say something. But Marcou remained invisible behind the sheet of water surrounding him" (82).[24] Here Marcou is surely evading his human responsibility, washing not just his hands but his whole body of the dirt that represents their human solidarity and their universal mortality. As before, Yvars waits for someone else to speak or respond, until it is too late for him to say what he thinks, but then, "Yvars dressed without washing" (83).[25] Just as he takes the little girl home with him, he takes the dirt from his day's work.

Once he is home, he finds release, "cleaned up in the wash-house" (83),[26] and only then can he tell the story to Fernande. In this final paragraph, as we have seen, many images come together for a final resolution: the weather, the horizon, the body, and the shared aperitif. In addition, Yvars, newly bathed, is seated on a bench while "mended washing hung about his head" (83).[27] Despite its being evening, the end is composed of images of renewal, of which the vain nostalgia for a lost youth is perhaps not the most important. Under the clearing sky and the clean laundry, Yvars does recapture some of the past: "He told her everything, holding her hand as in the early days of their marriage" (83).[28] At the factory, it is just this possibility of a return to the past and a new beginning that has been missing.

Camus's symbolism is thus pervasive but unobtrusive. He belongs in the modern tradition, of which Flaubert is perhaps the origin, where the symbols are never explicitly identified as such. They acquire their symbolic values through their functions in the story, weaving in and out at apparently significant moments, eventually forming a pattern of references. The reader is expected to supply meanings from another world, and these orient the reading of the text; and indeed, over the years, they will profoundly modify it. Nothing in such texts can be solely symbolic; everything must have a realistic place first.

Especially in *The Silent Men*, Camus selects his symbolic images from a humbler vision of reality than many other writers. To be sure, the Renegade is a figure worthy of Kafka, whom Camus admired, and *The Growing Stone* has some of the disturbingly mythic atmosphere of a story like *In the Penal Colony*; the silent old Arab on the parapet in *The Adulterous Woman* may remind us of the red-haired stranger in Mann's *Death in Venice*, just as the fly is probably a reminiscence of Dostoevski's *Crime and Punishment*. But apart from the Rene-gade, Camus shuns the grotesque and the bizarre, and there are not even many scenes or details that seem to possess that uncanny fitness we sense in the magic lantern at Combray or Plumtree's Potted Meat in *Ulysses*. Yvars's lame leg never has the impact on the reader of Hippolyte's clubfoot.

Nonetheless, Camus's stories often contain a central image; and if critics have been less sensitive to them, it is in part because of Camus's greater fidelity to everyday truth, and in part because of the critics' own misguided preoccupations. The center of *The Silent Men* is clearly the barrel factory, but critics have commented only on its biographical origins: Camus's uncle owned a barrel factory, and there is even a photo of the young Albert on the scene. Yet these barrels represent the men who make them. Yvars's lament for his craft stresses this personal, emotional connection. The men do not fear poverty and misery; other jobs could be found. A special kind of pride links them to cooperage, however: "You don't change trades when you've gone to the trouble of learning one; this one was hard and called for a long apprenticeship. The good cooper, the one who fits his curved staves and tightens them in the fire with an iron hoop, almost hermetically, without calking with raffia or oakum, was rare. Yvars knew this and was proud of it. Changing trades is nothing, but to give up what you know, your master craftsmanship, is not easy" (65–66).[29]

Indeed, one is tempted to call the coopers' attachment to their barrels "paternal." Certainly their loyalty exceeds the bounds of common economic sense, for rather than change jobs, they resign themselves to a humiliating defeat and an inadequate wage. The detailed technical descriptions of barrel manufacture convey more than the realistic background; they suggest something of the love and attention each man devotes to his work. The barrels are almost equivalent to children, and the deflection of the problem from the men's loss of their jobs to the boss's loss of his daughter insists on the comparability.

A terrible irony underlies the humanization of the barrels, however, for they have become obsolete. When there is no need for barrels, there is no use for coopers, either. These men are suffering from obsolescence even more than senescence. Just as the oversized factory building had grown emptier, so too the barrels now lie empty. The ancient symbolism of the barrel, source of bounty, has drained away, leaving instead the impression of hollowness. These shells are, of course, unmistakable images of soulless modern man, deprived of the inner meaning of life. The barrel is an appropriate symbol to these men in still another way. As Yvars's description makes clear, the highest skill of the cooper lies in uniting the staves. The barrel is an objective instance of solidarity, the separate parts fitted together into a functioning whole; in this, and in the cooperative fabrication, the barrel represents not only the individual but the group—the union. The bitterest irony of the story is that the blind course of history has rendered futile the noblest of humanity's qualities, that warm feeling of solidarity among the workers. Camus's position in *Exile and the Kingdom* is consistent, however; mass actions—whether political, religious, social, intellectual; whether emanating from state, church, school, union, or party—do not touch the heart of the problem. Nothing can restore the barrel to its earlier utility, nor the coopers to their earlier importance; and that is no one's fault. Moreover, even if time could be set back, it might not provide what Yvars—and presumably the others—most need: the happiness that comes of a full affirmation of one's humanity in an inhuman world, a world where economic laws will never be repealed and will always oppress someone.

As the title would suggest, silence is another key theme in *The Silent Men*. Cryle interprets the workers' silence as evidence of their simplicity; they adopt an attitude that becomes an embarrassment to them, but they cannot respond fast enough to the changing situation. In the end, according to Cryle, Yvars is "condemned to simplicity—and thus, in a sense, to incomprehension and injustice—because he is incapable of facing up to complexity and ambiguity."[30] As a reading of the psychological and social implications of the workers' muteness, this is satisfactory; but in almost all the stories, silence and lack of speech play an important role.

Janine, when she awakens in the night and begins to feel the call of the fortress, "was talking, but no sound issued from her mouth" (27).[31] Later, on her return, Marcel "spoke and she didn't understand what he was saying" (33).[32] No more does he understand her, and the story concludes on her ambiguous denial, "It's nothing, dear, it's nothing" (33).[33] It is not literally true that Janine and Marcel do not speak to each other, but Camus has told the story in such a way as to minimize the actual speech; at dinner, for example, Marcel seems "a husband suddenly taciturn unless he was telling how tired he was" (26).[34] His words are few in number, and betray chiefly his rather comic incomprehension of everything around him, including Janine. Her words are even fewer. Neither of them can understand the language of the Arabs among whom they live. The atmosphere is similar to that of Ingmar Bergman's film *The Silence*, where the soundtrack murmurs continuously in an incomprehensible tongue.

The Renegade has had his tongue torn out, and if he opens his mouth, "it is like pebbles rattling together" (34).[35] Throughout his feverish interior monologue, Camus interjects the nonsense syllable, "gra" to remind the reader of what Cryle terms "the paradoxical opposition . . . between logorrhea and the muteness of the hero."[36] An excellent article by Linda Hutcheon, dealing with "*The Renegade* as a 'new narrative,'" has pointed out the ways in which the Renegade's (false) interpretation of the black and white of the desert and his "garrulousness" apply to the writer's work.[37] Brian Fitch has proposed reading certain of Camus's other fictions, including *The Adulterous Woman*, as "new" in this sense.[38] In short, Camus surely meant muteness to have more than just its realistic meanings. It symbolizes something in his philosophical view of the world, including the artist's role. It is part of "an allegory of writing," present throughout these stories.

In its most obvious form, as a failure of human communication, silence expresses the individual's irremediable solitude. Yvars and the workers have not so much adopted silence out of pride as had it imposed on them: "their mouths had been closed . . . anger and helplessness sometimes hurt so much that you can't even cry out" (78).[39] Lassalle's attitude has reduced them to the status of things. Without possessing a lexicon of such terms of *reification* and *alienation*, the workmen nonetheless experience the feeling. They have been stilled like the machines of the factory.

The feeling of isolation overflows the gulf between labor and management, moreover. At the start of the day, the men are unable to talk even among themselves: "[The workers] were silent, humiliated by this return of the defeated, furious at their own silence, but the more it was prolonged, the less capable they were of breaking it" (70).[40] As work begins, still "all were working in silence" (72).[41] Even at home, the humiliation had poisoned relationships; the wives were sad, and Yvars had cut short his reply to Fernande—to her anxious question about the boss, "What will you men say to him?"—saying, " 'Nothing,' " and "his small, dark and wrinkled face with its delicate features had become hard. 'We're going back to work. That's enough!' " (68).[42] In a very mild fashion, Camus violates the point of view in that scene, which we see more from Fernande's perspective than from Yvars's.

As we have seen already, Yvars becomes more sympathetic than his co-worker Marcou because we know Yvars's thoughts. Inside views are inevitably seductive; we cannot help sympathizing with Yvars when we see through his eyes. By the same token, however, those whom we see only from the outside remain highly ambiguous. In many of the other stories, this ambiguity is emphasized by the perplexing actions that we witness. Did the jackal-soldier have any interest in Janine? Why did the lordly Arab advance straight at Marcel's case? Why did Daru's prisoner say, "Come with us" (101),[43] and why did he take the road to Tinguit? These extreme cases ought to sharpen our awareness of the problem in more conventional situations; Janine's husband is ultimately as great a mystery as anyone else, not reducible to some simple stereotype, the bourgeois, the colonial, or the male chauvinist. So too with the other characters in *The Silent Men*; nothing in the story explicitly invites one to imagine hidden motives or unusual depths in the other characters. We can easily supply plausible feelings for everyone, especially aided by Yvars's speculations. Yet they all remain radically Other, most particularly Lassalle, who disappears behind a door, keeping the secret of his grief and whatever effect the experience has had on him—not to mention the more mundane secret of what has actually happened to the little girl.

This Otherness is one of the devices Camus exploits most consistently to suggest his message at the end of the story. Ultimately, the narrator's voice must also fall silent, and we suddenly find ourselves before the character as an Other. As Yvars sits on his terrace, he pronounces a judgment on his boss: "Ah, it's his own fault!" (84).[44] What, precisely, was his fault? Presumably the workers' failure to speak, which has weighed on Yvars's conscience. Must we accept Yvars's verdict, or should we find him guilty of evading his responsibility especially in the light of his nostalgic escapism at the very end? And either way, has not Camus led us to do what Yvars has just done, and what all of them have done to each other? In other words, the fundamental problem of human relations that lies at the basis of the action is suddenly transposed at the end into a problem between the reader and the text. When the narrator becomes a silent man, we recognize that the text, too, is Other.

Nor is the person-to-person communication the only form that Camus calls into question. Once again, other stories raise much more dramatic cases, like Janine perceiving the mysterious writing on the horizon. The universe itself "speaks" to those who are willing to listen, but there are valid and invalid ways of hearing. The Renegade, clearly, illustrates an interpreter who forces the meaning; even Daru may be striving for an impossible purity and clarity of understanding—his four-color map of the rivers of France is strangely out of place in this arid, monochrome world. Yvars is a far humbler figure, who seems to have given up trying to understand; in the morning, at least, he simply refrains from looking at the sea, "always there to greet him" (64)[45] but which reminds him of loss, aging, and death.

As he pedals along, Yvars recapitulates the strike for us; his account is remarkably clear and impartial, and he blames neither his fellow workers, nor the union, nor even the boss. Yet though he presents the facts coherently, he is unable to reach any conclusion, other than his curt retort to Fernande, "We're going back to work. That's enough." As Cryle has said, in many other instances we see that Yvars's articulation falls short of the complexity of the situation, as in his unsuccessful effort to speak about the girl's accident: "Sometimes the word 'misfortune' took shape in him, but just barely, for it disappeared immediately—as a bubble forms and bursts simultaneously" (81).[46] Yvars's final line, "Ah, it's his own fault" is another inadequate conclusion. By contrast to the very lyrical, image-filled consciousness of Janine or of the Renegade, and also to the intellectual conscious ness of Daru or of D'Arrast, Yvars has a literal mind. As I have been arguing throughout, he lives in a universe full of symbolic objects and events, yet his own account of them barely hints at these implicit significances.

The author then must break the silence on two levels. He articulates to us the word *misfortune*, which Yvars could not quite formulate and pronounce himself; but he also presents the process by which the situation enters Yvars's awareness as "misfortune." He must give us Yvars's world, if not in its fullness, at least with greater resonance than Yvars perceives. Camus lends his tongue to Yvars, but at the same time to the inanimate world; in *The Renegade*, that image becomes explicit, for the Renegade claims to have a disembodied tongue working ceaselessly inside his skull: "something has been talking, or someone" (34).[47] There is, of course, an infinite regression of the series; for as soon as the word is spoken, it becomes part of that external "other" world. Camus's reading not only may be a misreading but also may be misread.

Silence is, then, one of humanity's first encounters with the absurd. The universe that we expect will tell us of the glories of God or at least of the wonders of nature is in fact a silent desert. Meanings must be forced from the world by a long and painful effort. In the final stories, Jonas and D'Arrast seem to have succeeded, through patience, devotion, humility, self-sacrifice, in overcoming the silence, and in the same stroke, in achieving some form of solidarity and happiness. The fanatical desperation of the Renegade, who actually tries to bite the stone (49), is one temptation of the artist; the lassitude of Yvars is perhaps the opposite. By the magnificent paradox of art, however, even the failures are transformed. The tongueless Renegade and the inarticulate Yvars both have their say, and the humanity of their encounters with the absurd pierces through the arrogant absolutism of the one and the pathetic simplicity of the other.

1. "Un Monde ambigu," in Jacqueline Lévi-Valensi, *Les Critiques de notre temps et Camus,* p. 98.

2. Pp. 101–18.

3. P. 102: "Il faut reconnaître que la présence des 'Muets' dans *L'Exil et le royaume* tend forcément à la rattacher aux autres nouvelles, riches toutes les cinq de résonances symboliques."

4. P. 1600: "Le hangar était devenu trop grand pour la poignée d'hommes qui l'occupaient."

5. P. 1595: "On était au plein de l'hiver et cependant une journée radieuse se levait sur la ville déjà active. Au bout de la jetée, la mer et le ciel se confondaient dans un même éclat."

6. P. 1606: "le ciel devenait transparent; par-delà le mur, on pouvait voir la mer douce du soir."

7. P. 1579: "Rien, rien encore jusqu'à l'horizon."

8. P. 1621: "au-delà, les terres invisibles qui s'étendaient jusqu'à la mer."

9. P. 1606: "ils seraient partis, de l'autre côté de la mer."

10. *Une Lecture de Camus,* 1977.

11. P. 108: "L'ouvrier n'a rien de la lourdeur engourdie de la bourgeoise."

12. P. 1595: "il roulait lourdement."

13. P. 1596: "Ce matin-là, il roulait, la tête baissée, plus pesamment encore que d'habitude: le coeur aussi était lourd."

14. P. 1611: "carré."

15. P. 1617: "s'il le fallait, il casserait en deux son adversaire."

16. P. 1655: "son large corps de colosse . . . affaissé par la fatigue, planté lourdement sur la terre."

17. P. 1559: "long et mince, si mince, . . . qu'il paraissait bâti dans une matière sèche et friable, un mélange de sable et d'os."

18. P. 1601: "mince et brun . . . il avait l'air à l'aise dans son corps."

19. P. 1604: "[La sonnerie] insistait, mais d'une si curieuse manière, avec de courts arrêts et des reprises impérieuses, que les ouvriers s'arrêtèrent."

20. P. 1603: "Tu m'inviteras à ton tour."

21. P. 1603: "Le malaise qui ne l'avait pas quitté depuis l'entrevue avec Lassalle disparaissait soudain pour laisser seulement place à une bonne chaleur."

22. P. 1606: "il lui raconta tout."

23. P. 1602: "Le premier mouvement d'Yvars fut d'aller se laver les mains, mais Marcou le saisit au passage par le bras et il le suivit en boitant."

24. P. 1606: "pensa que c'était à Marcou de dire quelque chose. Mais Marcou se tenait, invisible, derrière la pluie d'eau qui l'entourait."

25. P. 1606: "Yvars se rhabilla alors sans se laver."

26. P. 1606: "se lava dans la buanderie."

27. P. 1606: "du linge reprisé pendait au-dessus de lui."

28. P. 1606: "Il lui raconta tout, en lui tenant la main, comme aux premiers temps de leur mariage."

29. P. 1597: "On ne change pas de métier quand on a pris la peine d'en apprendre un; celui-là était difficile, il demandait un long apprentissage. Le bon tonnelier, celui qui ajuste ses douelles courbes, les resserre au feu et au cercle de fer, presque hermétiquement, sans utiliser le rafia ou l'étoupe, était rare. Yvars le savait et il en était fier. Changer de métier n'est rien, mais renoncer à ce qu'on sait, à sa propre maîtrise, n'est pas facile."

30. P. 118: "condamné à la simplicité—et donc, dans un sens, à l'incompréhension et à l'injustice—parce qu'il est incapable de faire face à la complexité et à l'ambiguïté."

31. P. 1570: "parlait, mais sa bouche n'émettait aucun son."

32. P. 1573: "parla et elle ne comprit pas ce qu'il disait."

33. P. 1573: "Ce n'est rien, mon chéri, ce n'est rien."

34. P. 1569: "un mari soudain taciturne, ou qui disait sa fatigue."

35. P. 1577: "c'est comme un bruit de cailloux remués."

36. P. 100: "l'opposition paradoxale . . . entre la logorrhée et le mutisme du héros."

37. "'Le Renégat ou un esprit confus' comme nouveau récit."

38. "Camus's Desert Hieroglyphics."

39. Pp. 1603-4: "on leur avait fermé la bouche . . . la colère et l'impuissance font parfois si mal qu'on ne peut même pas crier."

40. P. 1599: "[Les ouvriers] se taisaient, humiliés de cette entrée de vaincus, furieux de leur propre silence, mais de moins en moins capables de le rompre à mesure qu'il se prolongeait."

41. P. 1600: "tous travaillaient en silence."

42. P. 1598: "'Qu'est-ce que vous allez lui dire?' . . . 'Rien' . . . son petit visage brun et ridé, aux traits fins, s'était fermé. 'On travaille. Ça suffit.'"

43. P. 1617: "Viens avec nous."

44. P. 1606: "Ah, c'est de sa faute!"

45. P. 1596: "toujours fidèle au rendez-vous."

46. P. 1605: "Parfois, en lui, le mot malheur se formait, mais à peine, et il disparaissait aussitôt comme une bulle naît et éclate en même temps." O'Brien gives "calamity" for "malheur"; see my comment in the appendix.

47. P. 1577: "quelque chose parle, ou quelqu'un."

 Five

The Guest:
The Reluctant Host, Fate's Hostage

One character aids or shelters another who would normally be the former's enemy. This literary topos, which lies at the heart of Camus's *The Guest*, can be found in many versions, from folklore and legend to modern popular culture. It was especially popular with the romantics, in works like *Hernani* and *The Lady of the Lake*, and with other writers preoccupied with heroism, like Corneille and Saint-Exupéry. In these heroic versions, the guest's identity is often revealed late, and the host is presumed to be strongly motivated to harm the guest, even as he protects him in accordance with the laws of hospitality. Typically, the guest responds to this honorable behavior by promising to return for a second encounter between equals.

Camus gives us a distinctly modern variant, which could be outlined—still very abstractly—as follows. A schoolteacher in an isolated area is ordered by a policeman to keep a prisoner overnight and conduct him to jail. The teacher treats the prisoner kindly, offers him several opportunities to escape, and in the end gives him food and money and shows him the road to freedom. The prisoner, however, takes the road toward the jail.

Not only are schools, police, and prisons institutions of the modern state, but also the teacher's attitude reflects a very contemporary alienation. Policeman and teacher, agents of the same social order—indeed, both civil servants in this story—share no common sense of law. The conflict that was internal in the heroic versions has given way to a division of labor and the alienation that it entails. Yet the policeman and the teacher of the story are not enemies, either; they share a racial, cultural, and class background in contrast to the prisoner; and before the incident of the story, they had been friends.

With so bare an outline, one could imagine several reasons for the teacher's attitude: approval of the prisoner's crime, or belief that the prisoner had not committed any crime, or doubt that the prisoner would be treated fairly, or fear, or inability to carry out the orders. None of these, however, is the reason given by the story. The teacher, Daru, expresses no sympathy for the prisoner's act or any mistrust of the judicial system, and Camus has taken some pains to establish Daru's ability to do the job. He simply does not want to because he does not want to accept that responsibility. If he suffers from any inner conflict, it is of a sort quite different from the dilemmas of the romantic heroes, for he feels no desire at all to harm his guest. Despite the fact that the man has committed murder, Daru feels no obligation to participate in the process by which society attempts to deter such crimes.

The prisoner's last gesture, then, is highly ironic, a black parody of Hernani's vow to reconstitute himself prisoner of Don Ruy. It remains, moreover, unexplainable. As we shall see, many suggestions have been advanced to justify the prisoner's decision; but with the story narrated rigorously from Daru's perspective, there can be no fully persuasive explanation. In the earlier versions, the comparable twist in plot transformed this topos from mere episode to plot element by installing some weight from the past within the hero. Camus ends the encounter at this parting, but Daru's concern about the prisoner's decision reveals an involvement in it that contradicts his previous professions of indifference. Like it or no, he too has been weighted with the responsibility of the prisoner.

Camus, of course, added a final, uniquely modern touch of irony. When he returns to his school, Daru finds a threat written on the blackboard: "You handed over our brother. You will pay for this" (109).[1] This message contains still more mystery than the prisoner's actions. We never know the identity of its authors or their actual relationship to the prisoner; for "brother" can be taken literally, as blood kin, or more loosely, as an active member of some organization (a political party, for example), or more loosely still, as a passive member of some group (fellow countryman, for example). Why they prefer making the threat to freeing the so-called brother, an easy task under the circumstances, is not explained. And, of course, we never learn what happens afterward.

I have deliberately generalized this story before mentioning its most important particulars. Set in Algeria in the mid-1950s, it is the only story that alludes to the political crisis of the time. The prisoner is an Arab; Daru and the gendarme, Balducci, are both "pieds-noirs," Algerian-born of European descent. Balducci refers vaguely to the rebellious violence that led ultimately to the end of French rule in Algeria, and both he and Daru wonder whether the Arab might be a revolutionary terrorist, although they think not. Now, a quarter of a century later, Algeria has long since won its independence from France; but the real problem touched on has by no means disappeared. Given Camus's personal involvement in the early stages of debate, critics have quite naturally looked for political interpretations. In my view, this is a mistake. In revising, Camus consistently softened the possible contacts between fiction and reality. As the real conflict worsened, Camus made the story less and less precise. One could easily transpose the story into dozens of other settings without significantly altering its meaning.

To be sure, many elements drawn from reality support the basic story line. It is useful that racial, religious, linguistic, cultural, and class differences parallel the radical difference between an accused prisoner and everyone else—useful, but not necessary. Equally useful, at least for the moment, is the well-known existence of a liberation movement in Algeria; one accepts without question the rumors of a forthcoming revolt, knowing that in fact it came. But in how many places, in how many causes, have similar resistances occurred by now? A fictional underground would serve as well. We are accustomed by the events of our age to credit such things, including their most important trait, a certain irrational violence, born of weakness and anger. This trait, in the end, was as much a mark of the reactionary "Algérie française" movement, the clandestine secret army organization (O.A.S.) and terrorists of the right, as of nationalist or leftist guerrillas at the start. *The Guest* has nothing to teach about the Algerian conflict, except insofar as its problems were those of all conflicts, in all ages and in all places, between all sorts of people and for all sorts of reasons.

The question that inevitably preoccupies readers of this story is why the Arab takes the road east toward Tinguit, where the jail is, instead of the path south toward the plateau, where the nomads will provide protection. I wrote a short piece on this question myself in 1967, subtitled "A Note on the Value of Ambiguity."[2] Peter Cryle lists and refutes many critics of widely divergent opinions, including me; and there have been others since Cryle's book came out.[3] Roughly speaking, we can judge the Arab along four scales. First, and most basic I think, a passive/active scale: is he docile and dependent, or is he deliberate and autonomous? Second, a social/asocial scale: is he allied with an Algerian nationalist movement, or is he a loner, acting for personal reasons? The first two scales deal with questions of fact, although that does not imply that we can give a clear yes or no answer. The third scale concerns his placement in a social category: is he to be regarded primarily as a criminal, or as a victim of circumstances beyond his control? Within this scale would fall the matter of his guilt or innocence in the murder for which he was arrested, with all the extenuating circumstances that the judicial system recognizes; but also, more broadly, the possibility that French justice has intruded into a foreign domain, so that the Arab, having acted under one set of principles, is now to be tried under a different set that he may not even comprehend. Finally, the fourth scale of interpretation is really literary: is the Arab a hero—one who incarnates the author's conception of good or right behavior in some fashion— or is he a villain—one who denies the author's message or remains unaware of it and obstructs its accomplishment?

Each of the four scales can be applied independently of the others, so that there are sixteen possible characterizations, with of course a considerable range of shadings within many of them. Roughly, they can be arranged as follows:

The Arab as hero. In general, such interpretations look on the Arab's decision to go to jail as an effort to help Daru in one way or another. If the Arab is taken to be more intelligent and purposeful than he seems, then his choice is an existentialist's act of assuming responsibility. Whether he is a rebel or a loner, whether he is a common criminal or the hapless victim of an unjust colonial regime, he is sufficiently affected by Daru's fraternal attitude to be converted. His choice may represent an effort to please Daru, to honor Daru's system of justice, to dignify Daru's inevitable and unjust punishment. If, on the other hand, the Arab is taken to be ignorant, passive, and helpless, his final act is hardly a choice at all but a pathetic mistake. He may be trying to please Daru, or he may be so conditioned to dependence that he is afraid of freedom, or he simply may not understand and be taking the more familiar route. In any case, he means Daru no harm. If he has been a rebel, he must be trying to please an unexpectedly kind man. If the other was an existentialist reading, this one is liberal or humanist. Both Daru and the Arab (and even Balducci) are men of good will, trying to do the right thing, yet bringing misfortune on each other. The Arab's character, his passivity and ignorance, his possible rebelliousness and criminality, are creations of the government Daru represents.

The Arab as villain. The most extreme interpretation would make the Arab a conscious terrorist, who goes in the direction of Tinguit to deny Daru any sense of brotherhood; we do not know, after all, that he goes as far as the jail. One critic has suggested even that he turns himself in to provoke increasing violence, sacrificing himself as a sort of martyr for the revolution. It is perhaps more plausible to suppose that his "brothers" had planned an ambush along the road to Tinguit, and that he expects to rejoin them. If we consider the Arab as a loner, his motive must be simply an insurmountable hatred of Europeans. In any case, such readings can be characterized as extremist; they divide the characters into good and bad, and that division matches the division between European and Arab, between master and servant, between comfortable and impoverished, between policeman and prisoner, and so forth. From the bourgeois European perspective of the usual reader the following summary would be accurate: "to a Frenchman who gives him a great proof of humanity, an Algerian responds only with hate."[4] It should be noted, however, that an Algerian could equally well turn the extremist reading inside out; the prisoner's intransigent hostility would then be a heroic virtue.[5] It seems highly unlikely to me that Camus meant the characters to be separable into good and bad.

A more subtle version of the Arab as villain arises when he is regarded as a passive figure. Obviously, he cannot be held morally responsible in quite the same way. As a brutelike creature, killing a fellow Arab on blind impulse, seeking the easy way by instinct, he brings violence and hate in his wake. If we assume that he has become a political terrorist, we must suppose that it was because of his preference for easy answers. He goes toward Tinguit at the end, perhaps to rejoin his "brothers" along the way, perhaps to have a secure bed and three meals a day during hard times, but in any case untouched either by Daru's concern for his motives or by Daru's kindness. Daru, a kind of Camusian saint, has met his opposite and failed to awaken him to freedom. These readings are fundamentally pessimistic and tragic. The saints are few, the brutes many; and if the stupidity of the latter brings ruin to the former, there seems little hope that dreams of brotherhood could ever be realized.

Although the advocates of one or another interpretation will disagree, I do not find any explanation of the Arab's character and behavior satisfactory. Some are more plausible than others; but none is entirely without flaws, and none can be demonstrated false. Camus surely intended it that way. Daru does not understand, and we are to share his confusion, not view the events with an omniscient superiority. The presentation of the Arab in the story, scrutinized closely, confirms this ambiguity as intended. The Arab speaks only twelve utterances, totaling fewer than fifty words. Six are questions, three are imperatives, two are the single word "yes," leaving only the reply, "He ran away. I ran after him" to Daru's question, "Why did you kill him?" (100),[6] as a direct statement of the Arab's view of anything. The rest is all our inference, much of it influenced by Daru's own inferences. The Arab's eyes are "full of fever," his forehead "obstinate," his look "restless and rebellious" (90).[7] He watches Balducci "with a sort of anxiety" (93),[8] looks at Daru with eyes "full of a sort of woeful interrogation" (100).[9] In the darkness, the Arab turns toward Daru "as if he were listening attentively" (103);[10] and at their parting, the Arab takes the package "as if he didn't know what to do with what was being given him" (107).[11] Daru thinks he hears the Arab moan (102)[12] and thinks that he is escaping (103).[13] The Arab's expression the next day is "frightened," then "vacant and listless" (104);[14] twice he seems not to understand (106,107);[15] and in our final close view of him, "a sort of panic was visible in his expression" (108).[16] In short, Camus has been very careful to give us no authorial insights into the Arab, but to link every judgment of Daru's to a precise physical source. Daru is sometimes wrong, however, as when he thinks that the Arab is escaping.

The ending of the story appears to mean that, in some significant way, Daru has misapprehended the situation. Analyses that attempt to explain the Arab simultaneously attempt to explain the story by revealing the nature of Daru's error, and certainly a valid reading must focus on that error. Yet, as I have just shown, we cannot hope to solve the problem through understanding the Arab because Camus does not tell us enough about him.

The policeman Balducci is the only other character actually present in *The Guest*. Since he departs early, it would be structurally odd for him to represent the central focus. Nonetheless, he offers Daru a possible fraternal relationship, which does in fact go awry, at least temporarily. His role is worth considering, if only to see how it compares to the more important relationship between Daru and the Arab.

Balducci, of course, shares with Daru all those traits that separate the two of them from the Arab; no circumstantial barrier exists between them. Their past friendship has been close, almost familial. Despite being a policeman, Balducci expresses some misgivings about his role, and his attitude toward the Arabs is not unlike Daru's. He can speak some Arabic, he willingly agrees to untying the prisoner, he sympathizes with Daru's reluctance to hold the Arab: "I don't like it either. You don't get used to putting a rope on a man even after years of it, and you're even ashamed—yes, ashamed" (95).[17] Certainly he is not presented as a man who has forfeited his claim to fraternal solidarity with other men.

Before the Arab, Balducci represents responsibility to Daru. He brings orders from their common master, the French government. Even though he is unhappy about it, Daru readily accepts this responsibility by signing the paper. The understanding between the two men on this point is perfect. Balducci knows that Daru will tell the truth in any case, Daru accepts the fact that the rules require a signature. By signing, Daru releases Balducci and takes on the responsibility himself. At the same time, Daru refuses to follow the orders. He reaches that decision promptly and tells Balducci bluntly: "But I won't hand him over" (95).[18] Moreover, he repeats his decision twice. Balducci disapproves, but his own sense of obligation stops short of denouncing Daru. Their disagreement on the ethical question weakens the ties of friendship between them, but no misunderstanding occurs.

As Balducci leaves, Daru offers a ritual gesture of friendship: "I'll see you off," which the gendarme declines, saying, "There's no use being polite. You insulted me" (96).[19] Daru's refusal amounts to a criticism of Balducci's conduct. Their disagreement remains open and frank, however; canceling politeness keeps the superficial forms of their contact in harmony with its underlying truth. Between these two there are none of the false starts, words left unsaid, or half-gestures that characterize the relations between Lassalle and his workers in *The Silent Men*, for example. Balducci even softens his rejection somewhat, by saying, "Good-bye son" (96),[20] as he goes out. One feels that their long-standing camaraderie will not be permanently destroyed by the momentary conflict. Daru, it should be observed, neither contradicts Balducci nor apologizes for the insult. As with the responsibility for the prisoner, Daru acknowledges the disagreement readily if not gladly.

In short, Daru's relationship with Balducci comes near to being an ideal fraternal bond, capable even of surviving the inevitable troubled moments and crises that less-than-ideal reality produces. Critics who have blamed Daru for hesitation and indecision should reread the opening more carefully; Daru decides almost instantly to take responsibility for the prisoner but not to hand him over, and nothing in the story suggests that he is ever tempted to change his mind. The prisoner himself is too mysterious a figure for us to know with certainty how Daru ought to have acted, assuming that he ought to have done something different. A last critical resort has been to accuse Daru of some general complicity in his fellow Frenchmen's presumed guilt toward the Arabs. Daru, so the reasoning goes, represents an imperialist culture. He is master of his school, he feels like a lord by contrast to the poverty-stricken people around him. He is paternalistic, doling out the food and supplies, along with the civilization, shipped in from France. He is elitist, equating knowledge with the French school curriculum and imposing it on his pupils. Perhaps the best symbol of his clash with his surroundings is the map of French rivers chalked in four colors on his blackboard—the ruling country imposed on its subject, rivers in a desert, colors in a landscape turned black, white, and gray by the snow. It is the fitting spot for the threat to be written at the end.

Yet, though there is a certain symbolic justice in the desecration of the map, and a certain truth in regarding Daru as superior (in a pejorative sense), in human terms we must recognize that he has done about all anyone could to overcome his Otherness among these people. His feeling of lordship stems not from wealth but only from his acceptance of what little he has as enough. Undeniably he has had privileges of training and of comfort, but he is trying to share what he has and to give these poor people some of his privileges. Perhaps it is misguided to teach them the geography of France, although I see nothing to suggest that Daru does it with any spirit of condescension or of domination; I think that one must be frighteningly sure of one's own opinion to condemn him just for not knowing the best way to accomplish a worthy goal. Daru's treatment of the prisoner recapitulates his general attitude toward the Arabs. He insists on the prisoner's humanness, on his freedom, and on his equality with himself. They eat together and sleep in the same room, two rituals of fraternal bonding. Daru supplies the Arab with shelter, food, even money, and makes a small effort to educate him, not only about the route to freedom, but also, in asking about the murder, about moral responsibility. It seems from the changes in the Arab's expression and behavior that Daru wins his trust. Whether his gifts, his instruction, his kindness, his example of humanity succeed in making a lasting impression on the prisoner remains forever unknown.

In the end, there is nowhere to fix the blame and no place to locate Daru's misapprehension, unless it be that he misunderstands reality. He is a humanist in an inhuman or dehumanized world. He genuinely sees a brother in the Arab, but Balducci and the Arab's "brothers" can see only a criminal or a victim, a pretext for vengeance or a problem, an object within a system of objectified relationships. Daru is furthermore a respecter of ambiguity, who lives appropriately on the plateau between the desert and civilization, who wants to be a middleman between knowledge and ignorance, between plenty and poverty. But his world is growing increasingly polarized; one must be for or "against us," as Daru puts it, an act must be right or wrong, a person must be guilty or innocent. Daru is in many respects the most tragic, or at least the most moving, of Camus's heroes in *Exile and the Kingdom*, but he shares many traits with others, and especially with his immediate predecessor, Yvars.

All the first four stories of the collection are presented through the consciousness of a central figure. They all misperceive their world in some way at the beginning; all of them are relaxing in an illusionary certainty or habitual complacency, only to have their tranquillity disrupted by some unexpected turn of events. The stories end on the apparent alteration of the central figure's consciousness, but in terms of action, it is not very clear what this alteration portends. Janine's story contains the least drama in external events, the Renegade's makes the external world a scene of incredible barbarity and violence. Yvars and Daru occupy a middle ground, ordinary lives touched by an extraordinary event.

Both men, as they are initially presented, are decent and

likable. Yvars mulls over the strike as he rides to work, and his meditation leads him to justify everyone, including the boss who won and the union that refused its support to the wildcat strikers. Despite some anger and bitterness, Yvars's main feeling is sympathy for others, especially certain co-workers like Saïd who have suffered more than he has. Daru likewise appears first in a role where he sympathizes with others, his poverty-stricken pupils, the Arab prisoner, even Balducci. Both heroes are well-meaning, honorable, conscientious, and broad-minded.

The problem arises as an encounter with the Other: for Yvars, the boss; for Daru, the prisoner. Thus Yvars is an inferior looking up, Daru a superior looking down, yet their problems are the same: how to sustain a human relationship in a politically charged setting. Yvars has impulses of cordiality toward Lassalle and Ballester, but they are blocked by his awareness of the class barrier between them—an awareness heightened, of course, by the recent collapse of the strike and the workers' communal resentment. Daru's impulses of solidarity toward the prisoner are blocked by his disgust for the Arab's crime, which, under the French-Algerian government, has become his responsibility. Of course, Daru's position is in many ways more like Lassalle's than like Yvars's, and it seems plausible to imagine that Lassalle feels a frustration like Daru's in confronting his silent, "unreasonable" men. The Arab's unspoken feelings may well resemble the coopers': an insurmountable distrust and self-defeating humiliation before the boss or judge. In short, each one traps the others in their social or political roles, and feels trapped himself.

As they struggle to find practical ways to resolve an inner conflict, outside forces intervene to inject unintended meanings into their actions. Daru's prompt decision to free the Arab does not provide a code of behavior for their night together, nor does Yvars's return to work predicate the course of his day. As each one wrestles in silence with his conscience and his feelings, Lassalle's daughter is stricken and the Arab's "brothers" steal up to Daru's school. Suddenly Yvars's silence becomes a rejection, and Daru's becomes a police action. With our inner views of their minds and of the events, we can regard these interpretations as false. Viewed from the outside, however, they are plausible, even in a sense true. Both Yvars and Daru find that they have greater involvements with the Other than they had intended or realized. Indeed, there is a kind of role reversal for both: Yvars discovers that, in some circumstances, he, not Lassalle, holds the power to give or withhold help; Daru learns that he himself was the guest of the Arab in some ways.

The titles, with their possible multiple references, underscore this change in role. "The Silent Men" eventually seem to include Lassalle, reduced to silence by personal tragedy. "L'Hôte" is a wonderfully ambiguous term in French; it means either "guest" or "host" and could designate either Daru or the Arab in either function. *The Guest* is, in certain respects, a retelling of *The Silent Men* from the boss Lassalle's perspective. The gesture of fraternity goes unreturned, and the passivity of the Other is transformed by circumstance into hostility.

It is, in the final analysis, a silly romantic daydream to think that Daru could have done any more for the prisoner than he did. Can anyone seriously believe that Daru could have joined the Algerian nationalists who were fighting a guerrilla war against the French? Or ought he then to have accompanied the prisoner to the nomad tribes? It would have made no difference in the outcome. The threat was coming to Daru, regardless of what he did, and regardless of what the prisoner did. If there is any immediate connection between the prisoner and the "brothers," between the fate of the prisoner and the acts of the "brothers," that connection defies analysis, given the paucity of information available to Daru and to us. Daru's choice is between turning the prisoner in and setting him free. That is a moral choice for Daru, and he makes what is probably the right decision (although how many of us, given the chance, would free a presumed murderer?). The bitter irony of *The Guest*, which makes it the most bleakly pessimistic of Camus's stories, is that right moral choices do not change the world.

If there is a villain in *The Guest*, it is the same one as in the other stories, not a person or a society, but the universe itself. That is the truly silent, completely passive and indifferent element in every story. In many regards, the Arab is explicitly identified with this impersonal natural reality. His skin is "weathered" and "discolored by the cold," like the landscape (90).[21] Balducci refers to him as a "zèbre" and compares the murder to the slaughter of sheep (92–93).[22] All this recalls Daru's opening meditation on the region and the climate, ending: "The sheep had died then by thousands, and even a few men, here and there, sometimes without anyone's knowing" (88).[23] Later, he thinks again about the same general themes, and sums up the passage of history in the region: "Towns sprang up, flourished, then disappeared; men came by, loved one another or fought bitterly, then died. No one in this desert, neither he nor his guest, mattered" (97–98).[24] The Arab belongs to that eternal cycle, like the stones cracking in the sun, the stinging wind, the tireless waves, the wheeling stars, motifs that recur in almost every story. The Arab is just someone who passes by. His actions—the murder, his words to Daru, his staying at the school, his taking the road to Tinguit—signify no more than do the changes in the weather. If a mind and soul inhabit that body, they stay as unrecognizable as the mind and soul of the material universe.

Daru's error, then, is this: he had believed that his monastic life, his solitude, his love for others and his acceptance of his place, had created a harmony between him and his universe. The story ends on the line, "In this vast landscape he had loved so much, he was alone" (109).[25] He loved a landscape and nourished a delusion that it loved him, that in it he was not alone. He is, and always has been, alone in his moral existence. The honor he chooses to obey is his, not Balducci's or the Arab's, and certainly not the world's.

Looking back to my own earlier note on this story, I think I would not now use the word *ambiguity* to describe the theme or the situation. The Arab is not a puzzle we are meant to solve but rather a blank, eternally, irrevocably meaningless. It is pathetic that Daru becomes interested in him, and actually cares what road he takes, after Daru has any chance left to be involved. It is pathetic in the same way that Daru cares enough about honor to offend Balducci by refusing to go along with orders. Daru is a quixotic figure—Don Quixote too freed prisoners out of honor, and suffered for it later. But Camus's vision of the universe is a blacker one than Cervantes'. This confrontation between Daru and the universe is the very locus of the absurd. Daru lives through a pointless, meaningless, and unresolved incident, yet he invests it with a conclusion, fits it into a signifying system, and projects a resolution. Since we see it all through his eyes, we share his desperate yearning to make sense of it. Even though this longing may be an error, pathetic, quixotic, self-deluding, foredoomed, the human refusal to subside into purely passive insignificance is our glory, our one possibility of revolt against the absurd.

1. P. 1621: "Tu as livré notre frère. Tu paieras."

2. "Camus's Mysterious Guests: A Note on the Value of Ambiguity." It is distressing to realize how poorly I seem to have made my point, to judge by subsequent citations. I had written my commentary as a response to two previous articles in the same journal; both assumed the Arab prisoner to be an ignorant, helpless, passive victim. I made an opposite case to show that it was equally plausible, not that it was the right answer; but I have been recorded as one who believes in the Arab as terrorist. Peter Cryle attributes to me the view that "Daru has only to know the exact circumstances to see clearly what to do" (126n: "Daru n'a qu'à connaître les circonstances exactes pour voir clair devant lui"), and he quotes my sentence: "If he could truly know his Arab guest, know his guilt or innocence, he could make without difficulty the choice to free him or lead him to jail," with the comment: "The ambiguity of the situation is not a simple consequence of the lack of communication" ("l'ambiguïté de la situation n'est pas une simple conséquence du manque de communication"). If Cryle had quoted my next sentence too, "But of course, no one ever truly knows another, and yet we must all choose again and again," I believe it would have been obvious that I do not attach so much importance to the circumstances or to the lack of specific communication, but rather that I regard the situation as a paradigm of the universal human situation.

3. Pp. 119–48. For more recent articles, see Roelens, Rooke, and Womack and Heck in the Bibliography.

4. This judgment was offered by Franz Rauhut in "Du nihilisme à la 'mesure' et à l'amour des *hommes*," in Richard Thieberger, ed., *Configuration critique d'Albert Camus*, 2:39:"à un Français qui lui donne une grande preuve d'humanité, un Algérien ne répond que par la haine."

5. Comparable perhaps to the attitude of the French family toward the German officer in Vercors's *Le Silence de la mer*.

6. P. 1617: "Pourquoi tu l'as tué?—Il s'est sauvé. J'ai couru derrière lui."

7. P. 1611: "pleins de fièvre . . . buté . . . inquiet et rebelle."

8. P. 1613: "avec une sorte d'inquiétude."

9. P. 1617: "pleins d'une sorte d'interrogation malheureuse."

10. P. 1618: "comme s'il écoutait de toute son attention."

11. P. 1620: "comme s'il ne savait que faire de ce qu'on lui donnait."

12. P. 1618: "crut l'entendre gémir."

13. P. 1618: "Il fuit, pensait-il seulement."

14. P. 1619: "apeurée . . . absente et distraite."

15. P. 1620: "sans paraître comprendre"; "sans comprendre." O'Brien translates the latter as "blankly."

16. P. 1621: "une sorte de panique se levait sur son visage."

17. P. 1614: "Moi non plus, je n'aime pas ça. Mettre une corde à un homme, malgré les années, on ne s'y habitue pas et même, oui, on a honte."

18. P. 1614: "Mais je ne le livrerai pas."

19. P. 1615: "Je vais t' accompagner.—Non. Ce n'est pas la peine d'être poli. Tu m'as fait un affront."

20. P. 1615: "Adieu, fils."

21. P. 1611: "recuite . . . décolorée par le froid."

22. Pp. 1612, 1613: "On m'a dit de te confier ce zèbre"; the slang term *zèbre* is colorlessly rendered as "guy" in the translation. "Il a tué le cousin d'un coup de serpe. Tu sais, comme au mouton, zic! . . . " Ellipsis in the text.

23. P. 1610: "Les moutons mouraient alors par milliers, et quelques hommes, çà et là, sans qu'on puisse toujours le savoir."

24. P. 1615: "Les villes y naissaient, brillaient, puis disparaissaient; les hommes y passaient, s'aimaient ou se mordaient à la gorge, puis mouraient. Dans ce désert, personne, ni lui ni son hôte n'étaient rien."

25. P. 1621: "Dans ce vaste pays qu'il avait tant aimé, il était seul."

Six

The Artist at Work:
An Ironic Self-Portrait

Jonas, or the Artist at Work breaks with the pattern of Camus's other stories in several obvious respects. It is the only story set in Europe, and the entire action takes place in the Paris of the post–World War II cra. The events stretch over a considerable span of time, including several years at least; other stories recapitulate a life, but always within a carefully delimited present of one or two days. *Jonas* is therefore harder to summarize than the others, except in its barest essentials. Gilbert Jonas is the coddled child of a wealthy publisher; rather late in life he discovers a vocation as a painter and devotes all his energies to it. Meanwhile he meets and marries Louise, a devoted, intelligent, and resourceful wife. She finds them an apartment, despite the housing shortage; their architect friend Rateau helps make the inadequate space livable by ingenious fold-away installations. Louise and Gilbert have three children. Simultaneously, Jonas is discovered by art critics and dealers. The more famous he becomes, the less he is able to paint: would-be or actual patrons, disciples, visiting celebrities, dealers, critics, friends, and parasites (in addition to his family) take up more and more of his time, and force him to move his studio into smaller and smaller spaces. Eventually his vogue subsides, and his ability deserts him at the same time. He begins avoiding his family and friends, drinking excessively, and having tawdry affairs. Finally Louise confronts him. He is sufficiently remorseful to reform immediately, and builds a strange loft in the hallway of their apartment. There he spends more and more time, saying he is working but in fact meditating; by the end, he is staying in the loft all the time. At the very end, he paints a canvas with a word that is either "solitary" or "solidary," Rateau cannot be sure which; then he collapses, falls unconscious, and Louise calls a doctor, who reassures her that Jonas will recover.

All the stories in *Exile and the Kingdom* have ambiguous elements, and so it is not surprising that they have all occasioned diverse and sometimes contradictory readings. None, however, has given rise to such sharply opposing interpretations as *The Artist at Work*. At least one important point of fact has been questioned: many competent critics assume that Jonas dies at the end; others (myself among them) regard that view as a misreading, not as one of Camus's deliberate ambiguities.[1] When readers as reliable as Gaëton Picon, André Nicolas, and Dominique Aury all make the mistake, however, one must wonder whether the error does not reflect some truth, and we shall return to the question toward the end of this chapter. Obviously, one's conclusion about the tone and significance of the tale as a whole will be strongly influenced by whether one supposes that the hero lives or dies at the end; those who think he dies draw a pessimistic moral from the story, but they are joined by others who recognize that Jonas survives but still consider that he has failed in some way. On the other hand, several important critics, including Cryle, King, and Thody, see *Jonas* as basically optimistic.

In a less-pronounced manner, we have observed similar uncertainties about the conclusion of *The Adulterous Woman*, and we are in equally familiar territory regarding the biblical source. Jonas is the French form of the name Jonah, and lest there be any doubt about the allusion, Camus gave this story an epigraph: "Take me up and cast me forth into the sea . . . for I know that for my sake this great tempest is upon you (Jonah 1:12)."[2] Unlike "The Adulterous Woman," critics have at least tried to relate Camus's Jonas to his biblical counterpart, but the analogies are so general and intermittent that no single explanation has been agreed upon.

Jonas is narrated in the third person, as are four of the other stories, but this narrator is uniquely distanced from the story and the characters. Even though he keeps Jonas at the center of attention throughout, he does not limit his perspective to Jonas's. Rather, he evidences a certain irony toward Jonas as toward everyone else; and as Brian Fitch comments, this narrative stance is found nowhere else in Camus's works.[3] It gives *Jonas* a comic note that is absent from the first four stories of *Exile and the Kingdom*, and reminds one of a Voltairean tale. This humor also brings to mind Jean-Baptiste Clamence, the seductively witty protagonist of *The Fall*, which was originally intended to be one of the stories in this collection. In order to resolve some of the confusion and make sense of the anomalies, it seems reasonable to begin with the hero, and to analyze what Camus meant him to be.

On the surface, Gilbert Jonas resembles Clamence in many respects. At the peak of their careers, anyway, both seem to be perfect Camusian heroes. Both work in the service of humanity, the one as a man of law, the other as artist. Both earn wide respect and enjoy great success in all the most conventional forms—money, power, friends. Both men appear happy.

Yet their success, their happiness, even their virtues conceal, and to some degree depend on, less attractive qualities. Clamence, of course, comes to understand himself in a new light after he hears the mysterious laughter on the bridge. Jonas may not achieve any significant self-understanding; it is the ironic narrator who points out his weaknesses. Both are egocentric despite their apparent charity and benevolence. Jonas's generosity arises from his laziness, his indifference, his passivity; he simply cannot be bothered to organize his life. His wife Louise and his friend Rateau do it for him, insofar as possible, while he drifts unconcernedly along. Louise even does his thinking for him, to a significant degree, and this process extends even to his painting. Jonas's painting exists in isolation from his fellow artists and their work; it is Louise who "drags" Jonas to museums and exhibitions, and who remembers the names of the painters. Jonas "didn't quite understand what his contemporaries were painting" (116), and "had only a very vague idea of his own esthetic" (128).[4] Clamence, to be sure, never appears as

simpleminded as Jonas, and his secret lust for power contains
far greater potential for evil than does Jonas's naïve selfishness.
Nonetheless, in their heyday, both present the outward appearance of success and virtue while harboring improper motives
and exploiting other people.

For both men, success gives way to self-doubt and confusion.
In Clamence's case, he dates the decline in retrospect from a
precise moment, when he heard the laugh on the bridge. That
laugh, of course, reminded him of an earlier incident, a suicide
he failed to prevent. In any case, the decline is gradual;
Clamence begins to change his ways, to argue a different side of
moral questions. Then he tries to forget his anxiety in drink and
with women. Jonas does not look back over his career as
Clamence does, and thus never fixes a single moment as the
crucial turning point. Indeed, each step toward success brings in
its train some element of his eventual downfall. But Jonas does
not become aware of what is happening until the process is far
advanced. Long after he has really stopped producing, he still
says to himself, "I love to paint" (144).[5] Later, he deludes himself
that all he needs is "a good system" (146);[6] and as he starts to
drink, it is because "he had discovered that alcohol gave him the
same exaltation as a day of good productive work at the time
when he used to think of his picture with the affection and
warmth that he had never felt except toward his children" (147).[7]
This discovery contains no self-understanding, however; he is
still thinking that "he was going to paint, that was certain, and
paint better, after this period of apparent waste. It was all just
working within him . . . "(147).[8] Jonas abandons his debauchery
only when he sees one day the distress he has caused Louise. The
next day he constructs his loft, where he works until the end of
the story.

Clamence never recovers from his fall; he narrates his story in
a bar in one of the lowest districts of Amsterdam, surrounded by
derelicts and prostitutes. In this regard, *The Fall* differs sharply
from *Jonas*. At the same time, both men trace the same
movement at the end, withdrawing into a small isolated space:
Clamence into his room, where the last day's conversation

occurs, and Jonas into his loft. Both, moreover, have with them
a painting with a paradoxical message: Clamence has the stolen
panel of *The Just Judges*, around which he spins a complex web
of ironies; Jonas has his own canvas, with the single, ambiguous
word "solit/dary."

The plots, then, if one may call them that, offer many
parallels, as well as some important divergences. It is equally
significant that Camus has named both protagonists for proph-
ets. Jean-Baptiste Clamence, which is actually, according to the
narrator, a self-selected pseudonym, obviously alludes twice to
John the Baptist, "vox clamantis in deserto."[9] Other allusions
are numerous, including the cell of the final scene, where he
imagines himself arrested and decapitated, thus bringing to an
end his "career as a false prophet crying in the wilderness and
refusing to come forth." Many critics have discussed the biblical
allusions in *The Fall*, which obviously go far beyond the
character's name.

Jonas has posed more of a problem. As I have said, the
epigraph makes the allusion unequivocal, and most readers
accept the loft as some kind of analog to the whale. Father
Goldstain has also suggested persuasive similarities between
Jonas's simultaneously solitary art and solidary humanity, and
Jonah's solitary mission and solidary humanity.[10] Jonah was a
strange prophet; first he tried to evade his mission, and then
sulked because his predication worked so well that Nineveh
reformed and was spared. At the end of his brief story, Jonah is
alone in a booth outside Nineveh, and the Lord has had to teach
him again a form of solidarity: by evoking Jonah's sympathy for
a gourd, the Lord illustrates his own sympathy for Nineveh. In
short, the adventure of Jonah is twofold: he demonstrates his
solidarity first by self-sacrifice during the storm, but second by
the more positive acceptance of human brotherhood with
Nineveh. Both lessons are relevant to Camus's Jonas, whose
story incorporates both parts of Jonah's at the same time. On
the one hand, in the more famous part, Jonas's egotism nearly
destroys his family, but by entering the loft/whale he saves
them; on the other hand, his success as an artist wins disciples as

did Jonah's predication, but its very success undermines its meaning and isolates the artist/prophet, who retreats to a loft/booth.

In comparing Clamence and Jonas, we must also bear in mind that Clamence's great crime was precisely a failure to cast himself into the water. In fact, the epigraph to *Jonas* would seem much more intelligible if appended to *The Fall*. Clamence, of course, not only refuses to throw himself into the river when he might have saved the girl, but also avoids water ever thereafter. As he says at the end of the first day's talk, "I never cross a bridge at night" (15); and the book ends with his observation, "The water's so cold! But let's not worry! It's too late now. It will always be too late. Fortunately!" (147).[11] He is by his own admission a false prophet, and his name is self-chosen. Jonas, on the other hand, is a true name, and it would appear that he does accept his responsibility for the misfortune. One must bear in mind that Jonah did not know beforehand that the Lord would send the whale, and it is precisely in the short interval between Jonas's recognition of his errors and his construction of his whale that Camus has placed his symbolic leap into the sea, in terms, moreover, that point to *The Fall*. At the lowest point of his drunkenness, when alcohol has made him impotent, Louise asks Jonas if he has betrayed her, and he tells her the truth; "and for the first time, his heart torn within him, he saw that Louise suddenly had the look of a drowned woman . . . " (150).[12] Jonas resolves on the spot to reform; "The following day Jonas went out very early. It was raining. When he returned, wet to the skin, he was loaded down with boards" (150).[13] That soaking in the rain represents his plunge into the water, to save the drowning Louise. It too is a fall, but as with Clamence, the physical fall merely repeats a spiritual fall that had taken place long before; but what Clamence refuses and Jonas accepts, the human appeal from the water, leads in the end to a redemptive baptism. As we have seen before in *Exile and the Kingdom*, Camus uses water in its traditional role as purifier.

The lives of both Jonas and Clamence resemble Camus's own in too many respects for readers to ignore. In broad terms, the facile success followed by a stage of self-doubt and sterility characterizes Camus as well as his protagonists. *The Fall* and *Exile and the Kingdom* seemed to signal a return of creative energy, cut short, as everyone knows, by Camus's death in an automobile accident. Peter Cryle, who himself mentions a criticism apparently aimed at Sartre and found in both *Jonas* and *The Fall*, is nonetheless correct to insist on basic differences of tone. Brian Fitch cites additional points of correspondence, but again without wishing to make the two works sound identical.[14] Nor do I; but the self-portraiture constitutes a final link, and the differing results in the two works are important to note. That Camus portrays himself in Jonas does not mean necessarily that we must admire Jonas or even excuse him. There is obviously a great deal of self-satire in *The Fall*, some of it very bitter and despairing; but in the end, Clamence is not Camus, and what Clamence does is not to be imitated, nor is what he preaches to be obeyed. The satiric and ironic aspects of *Jonas* are gentler, and I see no cynicism in the character or in the narrator.

Yet Jonas is like Clamence in a number of ways. Although he comes to his senses before the end, he has been a false prophet. He has lived up to his name as a synonym for one who brings misfortune. As an artist, he has failed to fulfill most of Camus's ideals; Cryle terms him a "shameless survivor of a pre-Sartrian age" who has "no sense of responsibility."[15] He has no ideas about art, either, and, as we have seen, little interest in what other painters are doing. The real irony of his faith in his star is that he is right; pure luck has guided him, brought him friends, love, family, fame, money, success, without his ever having worked for any of it. In a sense, he is a pure fraud, a creation of the media. Cryle has commented that by using painting as Jonas's medium Camus avoids having to show us any examples of it. His vagueness is deliberate, however; Balzac or Zola writing about painters not only describes the pictures but explores the aesthetic ideas behind them. Without this conscious link between the world and the work, the artist is no more than a cipher.

For Camus, the artist has real work to do in the world. Thus the subtitle contains multiple ironies. As so often with Camus's titles, we cannot be sure whether it refers to Jonas or to the painting of Jonas called *The Artist at Work*. And if it refers to Jonas, how should we take it? Is his long decline into sterility his work, or the ambiguous painting he produces at the end? And if it is the painting of Jonas, who is depicted painting a portrait of a wealthy lady, is the irony directed against him, or against the society whose government sent a painter to consecrate that absurdity, or against artists in general for their betrayal of their mission? Perhaps *The Artist at Work* is as absurd a title as *The Just Judges*.

Camus gave only two of the six stories a subtitle: *The Renegade, or a Confused Mind* and *Jonas, or the Artist at Work*. Unfortunately (in my opinion), the English translation reduced both to a single title, the former by dropping the subtitle, the latter by dropping the title. In both cases, albeit for somewhat different reasons, Camus was alerting the reader to the duality of vision in the story. The Renegade's story is a pure first-person narration, rather like a stream of consciousness, since the Renegade cannot actually talk and has no audience, but at the same time logically and chronologically very coherent and structured. Like Clamence in *The Fall*, the Renegade is not entirely to be trusted, and the reader must be put on guard against him. At the same time, the two titles offer alternative interpretations; the treachery of a renegade implies more will than is suggested by a mind's confusion. Thus, in more than one way, Camus invites the reader to entertain contradictory views of the Renegade.

With Jonas, the duality of vision is equally remarkable, although the tone is utterly different. The style of *Jonas*, as Fernande Bartfeld quite accurately said, reminds one of Voltaire's tales.[16] Virtually all the devices of *Candide* or *L'Ingénu* appear in *Jonas*: the naïve hero whose faith and expectation encounters an indifferent universe, yet who repeats a consoling maxim long after its absurdity has become obvious; Jonas's star and his universal "Just as you say" echo Candide's "All is for the best" and his pursuit of Cunégonde. The comic-strip resiliency of Jonas and Louise likewise resembles a

Voltairean plot, although things turn serious at the end as in
L'Ingénu.

For both Voltaire and Camus, however, the primary source of
irony lies in wordplay. Both evoke a real world, recognizable to
the reader despite a constantly falsified description. Voltaire
even uses Oriental fantasy and science fiction, though clearly
intending reference to a real Paris of the eighteenth century.
Without the implicit contrast to our common sense of reality,
neither Micromégas's superior perspective nor Candide's naïve
one would be intelligible. Likewise, Jonas's world comes to us
distorted by the narrator, but in such a way that the language
still points to real referents.

One set of techniques emphasizes the impoverishing effect of
language. Objects are thrown together grammatically with no
acknowledgment of the meanings generated by their contact in
real life. The device may be a simple juxtaposition, as in
"supported simultaneously by the sentimental press and the
philosophical reviews" (115),[17] or a more flagrant antithesis, as
"The less he worked, the more his reputation grew" (131),[18] or an
anticlimactic series: "With the same enthusiasm, of course, she
entered that bed, then took care of the appointment with the
mayor, led Jonas to the town hall two years before his talent was
at last recognized, and arranged the wedding trip so that they
didn't miss a museum" (117).[19] Many other examples could be
cited. In every case, no apparent misstatement occurs; but the
sentence is designed to suppress the usual relationships among
its elements. The complex cultural links between philosophical
reviews and the sentimental press could be explained; their
absence from the sentence makes an incongruous and therefore
comic pair, and by the same gesture trivializes the ethical
principle under discussion. In the last example, the emotional
bonds of the couple have been ignored, as well as the relative
importance of the various stages of the courtship.

The final form of deliberate impoverishment is the literal
definition: "a disciple is not necessarily someone who longs to
learn something. Most often, on the contrary, one became a
disciple for the disinterested pleasure of teaching one's master"

(126–27).[20] Voltaire was a master of such periphrastic substitutions, fixing on the most improper elements of his targets and making those elements central. Camus uses the reductive procedure less than Voltaire, at least in this sense. Sometimes language misses the point and deflates; more often, it obscures the point and magnifies.

Jonas's father offers examples of both over- and understatement. He separates from his wife on grounds of adultery, by which he means that she spent too much of her time on good works; he decides to have his publishing house, the leading one in France, go in for specialization, by which he means books dealing with sex. It is obvious that such liberties make it possible to transform meanings radically. The landlords can think of their lucrative business as "real estate philanthropy" (120),[21] and an art lover can equate "on the decline" with "finished" (139).[22] These, and many other examples, are evident abuses; the commonly accepted sense of the term is violated by the application.

Ultimately, these tricks of speech, which appear comic in isolation, appear as habits or full systems. Jargon makes a brief display, in the phrase "indirect humanization" (127),[23] the term by which Jonas's disciples explain his work. Clichés are common. Repeatedly, in a way that reminds us of Janine and Marcel, or Yvars, the characters of *Jonas* attempt to express their complex situations and can do no better than reiterate some trite phrase. Louise justifies her (relative) neglect of Jonas, saying, "It can't be helped, each of us has his workbench" (118).[24] "A contract's a contract," says the art dealer, to prevent Jonas from donating a picture to charity (133).[25] The swarm of admirers who fill Jonas's apartment and interfere with his work are characterized by their self-serving aphorisms, such as "Lucky fellow! That's the price of fame!" (136)[26] or "Aw, go on! There's plenty of time" (144).[27]

Jonas himself is the principal culprit. His catchphrases, "Just as you say," and "This is the result of the star," both turn a formula into a means of evading reality. Most of Jonas's directly quoted speeches are similar clichés: "In art, as in nature, nothing is ever wasted" (126);[28] "After all, we never get a chance to see each other" (135);[29] "I love to paint" (141) (144);[30] "A little love is wonderful. Does it matter how you get it?" (145).[31] He even masters a complete repertory of encouragement and praise for his disciples (129).[32] These commonplace phrases serve in part to generalize Jonas, and make him express the average reaction to everything. At the same time, they reveal not only an astonishing shallowness in an artist but a serious moral weakness.

Many of the clichés function as euphemisms, constructing reality in the manner least likely to disturb the status quo. Sometimes Jonas acquires the clichés from others, as when he comments on an insistent and inflexible friend, "Isn't he thoughtful?" (124),[33] or makes excuses for his admirers: "Everybody is kind to me . . . many artists are that way . . . they're so lonely . . . you have to love them" (140).[34] Jonas is likewise taken in by the landlords and the art dealer. With Jonas, this banal Candidean optimism is a habit of mind as well as of speech. He feels gratitude for quite inappropriate reasons, and allegedly always has; for example, toward his parents, "first because they had brought him up carelessly and this had given free rein to his daydreaming, secondly because they had separated . . . " (112).[35] He is just as thankful toward the art dealer, the critics, the landlord, and more generally toward his "star" for such unlikely events as a motorcycle accident and the various obstacles to his work. Jonas has the logical pretext, which Candide does not, that until very late in the story everything has worked out well for him.

His language, however, has become a medium of evasion only. He differs from the hypocritical landlords and dealers in that he seems sincere, that is, self-deluded. His gratitude is presumably authentic, not a sociable pretense; so, too, his justification of his admirers, which offers no identifiable prospect of advantage to Jonas. Yet this self-deception is surely the most dangerous of errors, especially in the artist. Despite all the differences, Jonas here rejoins Janine, the Renegade, Yvars, and Daru, all of whom held comfortable false conceptions of the world they lived in. In Algeria, the sun or the desert can be counted on to force a heightened awareness on the Camusian hero; for Jonas, in the cozy comfort of Parisian civilization, the discovery of one's exile comes about in other ways.

Much of the comedy and satire in *Jonas* arises from the narrator's exaggerated mimicry of Jonas's foolish optimism. The narrator regularly adopts the most unreliable point of view as a source of his language, which he then repeats with no comment. The very funny account of the apartment is given almost entirely in terms that rationalize the landlords' exploitation of the housing crisis; the inconvenience to the artist from having an infant in his studio is masked by the perspective of an indulgent father; the impositions and occasional insults of the disciples are viewed through the complacent eyes of the overly tolerant and naïve Jonas. Rateau provides the only continuous counterpoint to the bland smugness; Rateau's resourcefulness and cynicism mark him as a literary descendant of Cacambo or Martin. Voltaire, however, lets Candide speak for himself most of the time; the narrator's voice is distinct from the characters'. Camus has chosen to tell most of *Jonas* in a sort of indirect free discourse, and as always with that technique, one can never be quite sure how much the narrator endorses what he says. Our perception of irony depends in large measure on our own sense of reality and justice, and our desire to exonerate the author of any wrongs in the tale.

In adopting this variable perspective, however, the narrator resembles Jonas; and though he is in no sense a dramatized narrator, the tone of his discourse further establishes their affinity. This story is uniquely entertaining, the work of a sociable man, a gifted conversationalist. Unlike the other stories, this one does not pull us into the dreary, limited world of a character but chatters brilliantly, as it were, over the heads of the characters—who are, in fact, much more like the probable readers of Camus than the others, and whose lives need not therefore seem so alienating. No effort is made to give us the sense of constriction in the Jonases' cramped apartment, or the despair of the increasingly neglected Louise, or the eventual breakdown of Gilbert. This story is distanced from the reader, and painless. The narrator's style is, in fact, very much like Jonas's, keeping everyone amused by avoiding commitment.

It has been observed long ago that the desert landscape has an allegorical value for Camus. The austerity, the hardness represent a form of clarity and truth. The hero, like Daru, tends to feel at home in this world of no illusions. The murky Amsterdam setting of *The Fall* is an obvious contrast, not only because of the fog, the dark, and the luxuriance, but also because it is a purely verbal world, spun out of the mouth of the witty Clamence, and perhaps not true. The Paris of *Jonas* is another such world, less evocative physically, for there is little emphasis on the setting, outside the apartment, and less obviously a verbal construction, since the narrator remains only implicit and never renounces his contract with the reader. Nevertheless, the narrator, like Jonas and like Clamence, is at home in this shifting world, where realities are mainly relationships—friendships, love, marriages, contracts, fame— that exist mainly in language; and everyone talks falsely. Philip Thody was right to speak of the feeling of relaxation in *Jonas*:[36] Camus is not struggling with the language to wring truth out of it, but letting it run its ordinary way. This is, of course, not to say that Camus has abandoned his consistent moral and literary intentions, only that he has tried a different tactic.

As an artist, Jonas possesses mastery over his medium, and earns, or at least receives, success. It is clear, however, that mastery of it is not the same thing as superiority over it. Success is not the same thing as lordship of the kingdom. Jonas's pictures fail spectacularly as a fraternal bond. His critics, admirers, and patrons have no more than a commercial or egotistical interest in him; only Rateau, on that side of the business, accurately distinguishes between the inessential picture and the essential act of painting. His aesthetic theory works no better; he cannot produce the picture of *The Seamstress* that might have made his pictures a real communication. Until his final collapse, painting has in fact been a barrier to Jonas. Learned too easily, accepted too naïvely, used too thoughtlessly, painting has done nothing more than make Jonas comfortable.

Language is no different, except that everyone uses it. For everyone in *Jonas*, including the narrator, instead of being the instrument that reveals, language is the habit of concealment. It can be compared to the shuttered apartment where Janine has spent her life, to the passive silence of Yvars, to the complacent paternalism of Daru, to the divine Word of the Renegade. Each of these ways of living, not evil in itself, collapses on contact with the harsh real world. Since Jonas's shelter is art, within the story he confronts the loss of that vocation. At the same time, Camus uses his own art form, language, to express the fraternal solidarity between Jonas, himself, and the reader.

Jonas's final painting is the concrete expression of this solidarity in several ways. Jonas paints language in the end, not images; in the most literal sense, his art rejoins the narrator's. As I suggested before, Jonas has abused language throughout the story, substituting clichés for realities, using conventional terms to avoid facing the many unpleasant truths of his life. Although he is surrounded by people who do the same thing, Jonas collaborates by passively adopting the other person's cliché or euphemism. Both with painting and with language, Jonas has been constructing his own isolation long before it happens in a physical sense in the story. In a curious way, the Camusian characters who live in the desert are fortunate; the truth forces itself on them. Jonas lives in a world without the hard stone, the brutal sun, the chill wind, the bitter salt of Camus's Algeria. When at length he recognizes the barrenness of his life, he must build a place of exile for himself, his loft.

The half-silence of the loft "seemed to him the silence of the desert or of the tomb" (153),[37] but Jonas begins his rebirth there, as do the other protagonists. He tells his friend Rateau, "I'm working," although as the narrator immediately makes clear, "He was not painting, but he was meditating" (152).[38] Meditation is work for the artist, and, in fact, only during these final pages, when he is in the loft and not actually painting, does Jonas say insistently that he is working. His proper work is to come to terms with his real condition, alone but among his own people.

It is obvious how the loft makes real the philosophical status of Jonas, like Janine's parapet, Yvars's balcony, Daru's plateau, or the Renegade's lookout. Superior and distant enough to permit a detached contemplation, but close enough to maintain some contact, all these lofts symbolize to a degree the paradox of solitary and solidary. They also belong within the individual stories to other sets of spaces, some prisonlike, some homelike, others terrifyingly or liberatingly open, and in most cases possessing paradoxically conflicting resonances for the character and for the reader.

In the loft, the blank canvas becomes the mysterious space of the desert, where the other protagonists trace a message. For Jonas as for the others, silence becomes the chief signifier of solitude, and the canvas represents the pure exile of speech. Painting ought to be mute, and Jonas's vocation ought therefore to have kept him free from the lies of language. Plainly, it has not—no more than the muteness of boredom in Janine's case, of pride in Yvars's, of monasticism in Daru's, or of barbaric mutilation in the Renegade's.

When Jonas's meditation comes to an end, then, he must return to the world of language. Many paradoxes are resolved at once in a single symbol, naïvely obvious like the loft itself, but solid and clear. All human communications are one, all human situations are one, solidary and solitary are one. The ambiguity of language, heretofore a source of deception, becomes the medium for a serious message.

It is important to remember, however, that it is a vision, not a saying. Jonas re-creates, re-presents; his word was never a prescription, or even a description, but a rendering of something perceived. Like the other heroes, Jonas has had to give up comforting certainties of all kinds and accept life in a world of uncertainties. His star never existed; what he sees toward the end may be the after-image of the lamp, the gleam of a chink in his loft, or simply a hallucination, but it is his only as the product of his own mind. Here again Jonas recalls Janine, falling in a swoon beneath the wheeling stars. Jonas likewise finds his star again by recognizing the indifference of the cosmos and accepting his place within it, not by reviving his smug confidence that providence was guiding him. His recovery from despair results from his own work.

That strange painting is the final version of *The Artist at Work*, capturing the full ambiguity of that status. Jonas the character and *Jonas* the story are versions of *The Artist at Work*, as are finally all the stories. Each one in its own way gives a material representation to the dual nature of human existence, both solitary and solidary; each shows the individual as artist in the effort, however feeble or belated or misguided, to transform solitude into solidarity through communication; each in some form makes perceptible the author's function as artist within the story, using his own special privilege to effect that transformation.

With *Jonas* as with the others, the story ends without complete resolution. The doctor is categorical: "He will get well." A literal death has surely not occurred. But what of the doctor's other comment: "He is working too much" (157)?[39] We are back in the land of cliché and empty rhetoric, and Jonas's future is as dubious as Janine's or Daru's. He has passed through a symbolic death, at least; the silence was not only like the desert but also like the tomb. He may be reborn transformed by his experience and incapable of painting; or he may have recovered his inspiration in rediscovering his star. The latter would seem to be Camus's intention; but it seems certain that the new Jonas will not enjoy the worldly success of the old. The artist's popularity was a delusion of human solidarity, and in reality the worst of exiles. The reborn Jonas must stay faithful to his own work. If there is a star, he must follow it, and not expect it to follow him.

1. Cryle calls it "une erreur de lecture" (p. 171); see his chapter, pp. 149–74, for a more complete account of critical debate on *Jonas*.

2. P. 1625: "Jetez-moi dans la mer . . . car je sais que c'est moi qui attire sur vous cette grande tempête."

3. "*Jonas* ou la production d'une étoile," p. 63.

4. Pp. 1630, 1636: "comprenait mal ce que peignaient ses contemporains"; "n'avait qu'une idée obscure de sa propre esthétique."

5. P. 1645: "J'aime peindre."

6. P. 1646: "une bonne organisation."

7. P. 1647: "Il avait découvert que l'alcool lui donnait la même exaltation que les journées de grand travail, au temps où il pensait à son tableau avec cette tendresse et cette chaleur qu'il n'avait jamais ressenties que devant ses enfants."

8. P. 1647: "Il allait peindre, c'était sûr, et mieux peindre, après cette période de vide apparent. Ça travaillait au-dedans, voilà tout."

9. P. 147; other references will be given in the text. The French, from the same volume as *L'Exil et le royaume*, p. 1549: "ma carrière de faux prophète qui crie dans le désert et refuse d'en sortir." The biblical quotation is from Matt. 3:3.

10. "Camus et la Bible."

11. Pp. 1481, 1549: "je ne passe jamais sur un pont, la nuit." "L'eau est si froide! Mais rassurons-nous! Il est trop tard, maintenant, il sera toujours trop tard. Heureusement!"

12. P. 1648: "Et pour la première fois, le coeur déchiré, il vit à Louise ce visage de noyée."

13. P. 1648: "Le jour d'après, Jonas sortit très tôt. Il pleuvait. Quand il rentra, mouillé comme un champignon, il était chargé de planches."

14. Cryle, p. 151; Fitch, "*Jonas* ou la production d'une étoile."

15. P. 150: "Survivant éhonté d'une ère pré-sartrienne, Jonas n'a aucun sens de la responsabilité."

16. "Les Paradoxes du *Jonas* de Camus."

17. P. 1629: "à la fois soutenue par la presse du coeur et les revues philosophiques."

18. P. 1638: "Sa réputation, par chance, grandissait d'autant plus qu'il travaillait moins."

19. P. 1630: "Du même élan, aussi bien, elle entra dans ce lit, puis s'occupa du rendez-vous avec le maire, y mena Jonas deux ans avant que son talent fût enfin reconnu et organisa le voyage de noces de manière que tous les musées fussent visités."

20. P. 1636: "un disciple n'était pas forcément quelqu'un qui aspire à apprendre quelque chose. Plus souvent, au contraire, on se faisait disciple pour le plaisir désintéressé d'enseigner son maiître."

21. P. 1632: "la philanthropie immobilière."

22. P. 1642: "Un artiste qui baisse est fini."

23. P. 1636: "humanisation indirecte."

24. P. 1631: "Tant pis, chacun son établi."

25. P. 1639: "Un contrat est un contrat."

26. P. 1641: "Heureux gaillard! C'est la rançon de la gloire!"

27. P. 1645: "Bah! Tu as bien le temps!"

28. P. 1635: "En art, comme dans la nature, rien ne se perd."

29. P. 1640: "Finalement, on ne se voit plus."

30. PP. 1644, 1645: "J'aime peindre."

31. P. 1645: "Un peu d'amour, c'est énorme. Qu'importe comme on l'obtient."

32. P. 1637.

33. P. 1634: "Est-il gentil, celui-là!"

34. P. 1643: "Tout le monde est gentil avec moi . . . beaucoup d'artistes sont comme ça . . . ils sont seuls . . . il faut les aimer."

35. Pp. 1627–28: "d'abord parce qu'ils l'avaient élevé distraitement, ce qui lui avait fourni le loisir de la rêverie, ensuite parce qu'ils s'étaient séparés. . . . "

36. *Albert Camus 1913–1960*, p. 192.

37. P. 1649: "lui paraissait celui du désert ou de la tombe."

38. P. 1649: "Il ne peignait pas, mais il réfléchissait."

39. P. 1652: "Il guérira. . . . Il travaille trop."

 Seven

The Growing Stone:
Reconciliation and Conclusion

The Artist at Work broke the pattern of the first four stories in
several ways; it used a new narrative perspective, it covered an
entire life rather than a single day, it was set in Paris rather than
North Africa. The final story also departs from the original
pattern in some of the same ways. In its simplest outline, *The
Growing Stone* relates the arrival of an engineer in an isolated
town and his acceptance by the townspeople. The engineer,
D'Arrast, is French; the town, Iguape, is in Brazil. The story
opens with an extended account of the trip to Iguape, in a car
driven by a native of the region, named Socrates; the most
remarkable incident is crossing a river on a primitive ferry. In
the town, D'Arrast meets the notables, the Mayor, the Judge,
the Harbor Captain, and the Chief of Police, who makes trouble
over D'Arrast's passport. He then visits the poor area near the
river, where he is to design a flood control dike. There he meets a
Cook, who becomes a key figure. Iguape has a shrine, centered
around a miraculous stone that grows; and the church has a
statue of Jesus, which arrived by "swimming" upstream. The
Cook has made a vow to carry a large stone to the church in a
procession, but he succumbs to his love of dancing the night
before and is too weak to fulfill his promise. D'Arrast picks up
the stone and carries it past the church to the Cook's hut, where
he places it in the center of the room. The Cook's family invite
him to sit down with them.

This summary, despite its brevity, gives some idea of the comparatively cluttered action. Peripheral characters abound; numerous incidents remain unresolved, although the action is spread over a span of several days. The unifying thread is, of course, D'Arrast; but it is not his desire or will that propels the plot. He has come on a mission, yet the story ends before he has really begun his work. He asserts himself in various ways: he asks to visit the poor section, he insists that the Police Chief not be punished, and he seizes the Cook's stone. Yet in a sense, he is almost pure consciousness, for he seems to have no memories, no feelings, no expectations. In the face of such disturbances as the drunken Police Chief's threats, or the hostility of the old Negro whose hut he is shown, or his exclusion from the dance, D'Arrast's cool tranquillity reminds one of the legendary heroes of the Hollywood Western.

The Brazilian setting, itself an anomaly, puts these events in a context radically different from the North African stories. Where they were arid and lonely, Iguape is humid and teeming with life of all kinds, including people. Even Jonas does not encounter as diverse a group, and the crowds in his apartment remain anonymous ciphers, whereas the Iguapeans assume vivid and individual lives in *The Growing Stone*. In part, this results from D'Arrast's insistence on visiting the humblest part of town and from his ability to talk to people like his chauffeur or a cook. Even before D'Arrast articulates his comprehensive interest in humanity, however, the reader can sense a new kind of fraternal feeling, in the evocation of the ferryboat men or the Japanese living in the jungle. There is an extraordinary babble of voices and languages around D'Arrast, and a mixture of nationalities, races, and classes.

D'Arrast moves into this world with almost perfect freedom. Although he recalls a recent crisis, in terms that link him to other characters, he remains unencumbered by it. Neither guilt nor frustration surfaces in his thoughts. Moreover, he shows as little concern for the future as for the past. He has come to build a dike, but expresses no impatience to get started. He manifests no desire to return home to France, either. This description makes him sound completely passive, but that is inaccurate; he possesses a great deal of energy and, in certain key situations, takes initiatives. Understanding the story depends largely on identifying the peculiar qualities of those situations. D'Arrast is free, like the heroes of eighteenth-century philosophical tales. Camus has left him undetermined so that he may act freely and, in that freedom, confront the moral issues that the other characters found thrust upon them.

In the foreground of the story are the relations between D'Arrast and the people of Iguape. D'Arrast never suffers the kind of isolation that becomes the lot of the Renegade or Daru, and the end of the story shows him being invited to join a group, as the beginning had shown him on comradely terms with Socrates. This easy sociability does not mean that his contacts with others arise automatically, however, or that they encounter no obstacles. Even the genial Socrates has an annoying, though involuntary, trait: he keeps D'Arrast from sleeping with his "cataclysmic" sneezing (168).[1]

D'Arrast's friendship with the Cook grows under still more trying circumstances. At their first meeting, when the Cook tells about his vow, "D'Arrast felt slightly annoyed" (185),[2] but he agrees to participate in the ceremony anyway. By evening, when they go to the dancing together, they seem to be on close terms, but the Cook jeopardizes that closeness by sending D'Arrast away. He addresses him "coldly, as if speaking to a stranger," and tells him "they don't want you to stay now" (197).[3] Furthermore, the Cook reneges on his resolution not to dance and rebuffs D'Arrast, who had been invited partly to help him keep the promise. D'Arrast sustains and even imposes the fraternal solidarity between them by ignoring these slights and committing his own energies to what he takes to be the most genuine of the Cook's desires.

The Cook serves in part to represent a special community, the Negroes who live in the huts by the river and who are the most impoverished citizens of Iguape. At first, D'Arrast's efforts to make contacts among them are met with hostility. Only because the Harbor Captain speaks to the Negroes "in a tone of command" (175)[4] is D'Arrast able to gratify his desire to visit one of the huts. When no volunteers come forward, the man to whom the order is delivered obeys it with a hostile look. And it is in the name of the whole community that the Cook requests D'Arrast to leave the dance.

To outward appearances, the Police Chief raises a more daunting challenge. He wears the uniform of authority, and his demand that D'Arrast show his passport would ordinarily presage continual harassment. In fact, he is made to back down almost instantly by the Judge; but for D'Arrast a new problem arises immediately in place of the first: the Judge insists that D'Arrast decide on a punishment for the Police Chief. D'Arrast temporizes, and tries to evade the responsibility; the Judge reminds him several times, however, and requires that he pronounce a sentence. Ultimately, D'Arrast finds the solution in a graceful speech appealing for leniency as a special favor so that his stay in Iguape "could begin in a climate of peace and friendship" (188).[5]

The incident has no further repercussions. Its arbitrary inclusion calls attention to its importance for Camus as a final statement on the theme of justice. We never learn why the policeman behaved so boorishly, except that he was drunk; but if that is the whole explanation, we never learn why the citizens so urgently demand that he be punished. It is a virtually pure exercise in judicial reasoning, thrust upon D'Arrast by the circumstances. D'Arrast, unlike Daru, rises to the occasion. He finds the formula that will both accomplish his wish, that the offender be pardoned, and satisfy the legitimate need of the community to affirm its laws. He finds within the ethical code of the Iguapeans themselves the pretext for the pardon, and at the same time assumes full responsibility for the judgment. It was precisely this gesture that Daru failed to make, either for Balducci or for the Arab.[6]

Once that hurdle has been cleared, however, D'Arrast finds no barriers to communication with the wealthy and powerful citizens. All of them except the Police Chief had welcomed him enthusiastically from the start, and once the Judge has pronounced his verdict acceptable, D'Arrast enjoys the full favor of the community. Instead of settling comfortably into it, D'Arrast moves on to the sterner challenge of the poor people in the huts.

When, from his vantage on the balcony, he sees that the Cook has faltered, D'Arrast leaves the company of the notables and rejoins the common people in the crowd. He takes the Cook's burden on his own shoulders, but he does not exactly fulfill the Cook's vow. He passes by the church and instead carries the stone to the Cook's hut.[7] There he awaits the decision of the Cook's family and friends whether his action has earned him acceptance or not. The verdict is again favorable; he is invited to sit down among them. Once more, D'Arrast has succeeded in meeting the standards of the society around him without betraying his own convictions. He has not pretended to have a faith he lacks, and has graphically shown that his own faith is in people. At the same time, he has taken seriously the beliefs of the others, and shared their sense of responsibility if not the faith behind it. Consequently, he achieves the fraternal union that he sought, by reconciling his values and theirs.

The bonds that D'Arrast forms between himself and other individuals represent possibilities of fraternal links across many kinds of social barrier. In virtually every story, the main characters are isolated by the most ordinary differences. They belong to different races or civilizations or economic classes from the people around them. D'Arrast shares all these signs of difference. He comes to Iguape as an exemplar of European civilization, with all that implies of knowledge and power. His sole reason for being there is to put his superior skill as an engineer at the service of a less-advanced society. Of course, both Daru and the Renegade intended to carry out similar missions. The risks of misunderstanding are great, as the industrial nations have learned to their dismay in the real world. The benefits of technology and material gains seem worthless if they must be purchased through self-abasement.

D'Arrast must, then, offer his superior skills without making the beneficiaries feel inferior. Perhaps it is for this reason that Camus so completely neglects the actual construction project for which D'Arrast has come. The engineer begins by trying to learn about, and from, the people of Iguape. The significance of the name Socrates also becomes clear in this context. Despite the initial impression of comic irony, the name should be taken seriously as designating a wise man. The traditional wisdom of the Greek Socrates was to pretend ignorance and question others. The Brazilian Socrates embodies a genuine wisdom in his relative ignorance, and D'Arrast becomes his disciple, a seeker, not a dispenser, of the truth.[8]

It is in very similar fashion that D'Arrast resolves the judicial problem, as we have just seen. For the European, D'Arrast's leniency expresses the highest ideals of liberal justice, whereas the local citizens' demand for punishment seems vindictive and harsh. So it may be, but we may not assume the moral superiority of "ours" over "theirs," of civilization over primitive society. In the end, they prove to be quite capable of encompassing a pardon within their own code, and this resolution of the question of justice is simultaneously a reconciliation of the two civilizations.

Of all the difficulties that D'Arrast must confront, none poses more profound challenges than religion. Class, language, race, or wealth might seem in the real world to be the chief obstacles to human solidarity. From the perspective of the Camusian hero, however, these problems are illusory; it suffices for the person with the apparent advantage to put aside prejudice, in order for the real equality of all people to become manifest. The European's superior technical knowledge was actually a graver difficulty; the engineering skill of D'Arrast is no illusion. In this case, however, the barrier can still be overcome because the technician and the ordinary people share the same sense of purpose. It seems less plausible that they should find a shared sense of faith. Camus's anxious pursuit of the truth about humanity's place in the universe led to a passionate skepticism that seems incompatible with sophisticated liberal religions, much less with the Cook's superstitious faith.

Yet even here, D'Arrast achieves a reconciliation, in part because he listens respectfully to the Cook's ideas about God, but also because the Cook's faith strangely resembles Camus's skepticism. The Cook's religion provides no dogmatic answers to the questions that haunt Camus. The universe retains all of its capricious indifference to human needs, and the good Jesus answers prayers according to his own inscrutable judgments.

With so honest a recognition of the truth, the Cook's superstitions about miracles and vows appear no more than a naïve formulation of the very problems that concern D'Arrast, and Camus—how human beings fit into the world around them, and how they can act responsibly. The local priest is conspicuously absent from the group of dignitaries who welcome D'Arrast, and with whom D'Arrast establishes the first cordial relations. The reconciliation with religion is not achieved with the likes of the Renegade, or Father Paneloux or the prison chaplain from Camus's earlier works. It is only with a simple man, as direct and honest in his faith as D'Arrast in his unbelief, that this last division between people can be closed.

The severest trial occurs at the Negroes' dance, which is actually a religious ritual reminiscent of the Taghâsans' fetish worship. The dancers' hut shelters an altar with "a magnificent colored print in which Saint George, with alluring grace, was getting the better of a bewhiskered dragon" (190).[9] Even in this apparently Christian image, violence predominates. Beneath the altar, however stands a little statue "representing a horned god . . . with a fierce look . . . brandishing an oversized knife made of silver paper" (191).[10] Obviously the faith of the Iguapeans spans the whole range from savage ancient deities to modern Christianity. As the ceremony progresses, these hints of blood-shed are realized when the dark girl appears, as a central figure in the dance, holding "a green-and-yellow bow with an arrow on the tip of which was spitted a multicolored bird" (196).[11]

Many elements of the ceremony resemble scenes from the hut of the fetish in Taghâsa, beginning with the rhythmic dance. In Iguape as in the city of salt, the people are transformed into animals, uttering inarticulate sounds, shrieks, howls, and "a strange bird cry" (196).[12] One woman, "rolling her animal face from side to side, kept barking" (194).[13] The participants enter into a collective frenzy, they are "possessed of the spirit" (193),[14] they fall to the floor in exhaustion. Some are masked, and all, even the Cook, are transfigured into distorted forms. In their own view, they become "the god's field of battle" (193),[15] and the double axhead of the fetish reappears as the short saber wielded by the Negro dancers.

D'Arrast's place in this ceremony is problematic. He is, to be
sure, an outsider. Almost as soon as he arrives, he is singled out
by the leader as an impediment: "Unfold your arms . . . you are
hugging yourself and keeping the saint's spirit from descending,"
the Cook explains to him (191).[16] D'Arrast complies, and
perhaps there is a grain of truth in the implicit criticism of his
egotism and withdrawal. Immediately afterward, D'Arrast
begins to resemble a "bestial god" himself, albeit a kindly one
(192).[17] He remains pressed against the wall, like the Renegade,
drawn unconsciously into the communal experience at moments, but excluded from real participation. The heat and
smoke nauseate him, as the bitter drink had sickened the
Renegade. Finally he is rejected by his guide and ordered to
leave.

We must not, of course, push the parallel between D'Arrast
and the Renegade too far. D'Arrast is never beaten or mutilated
or physically mistreated in any way. The similarities permit us to
make some connections, but not to equate the two. D'Arrast is,
in fact, a false victim, almost a decoy. He could have made his
plight worse by stubborn resistance or by self-pity, but as we
have seen, he characteristically accepts rebuffs and frustrations
with equanimity. And indeed, the real victim of the ceremony is
not D'Arrast but the Cook.

The Cook has already once been designated as the symbolic
scapegoat, when he was drowning. He was rescued then, he
believes, by the good Jesus, to whom he made a vow. At the
dance, he gives in to his love of dancing, to the cigars, to the
eroticism; and the next day he cannot fulfill his vow. The ritual
has been a trap for him, and in his own mind it has caused him
to be cast back into the sea. In the procession, we recognize him
as the victim again, for he is dying of the effort to carry the
stone, and resembles Christ carrying the cross. This time, only
when D'Arrast intervenes is the fatal sacrifice thwarted.

D'Arrast survives the ritual because of his respect for others.
Unlike the Renegade, he had not come to convert these people.
Whatever he may think of the cult of Saint George or the horned
god, he feels no need to impose his beliefs on the celebrants.

When told to unfold his arms, he offers no resistance; when ordered to leave, he goes willingly. He accepts as much participation as the poeple will allow him and demands no more.[18]

The next day, at the procession, however, he seizes a role. By relieving the Cook, he assumes for himself the function of the scapegoat. At the same time, he asserts a new doctrine; for when he bypasses the church, he changes the nature of his gesture. Instead of laying the stone, and his exhausted body, as a sacrifice before the sacred altar, he returns the stone to the midst of the people and actually makes a new altar of it. Symbolically, a new order has been founded, no longer dependent on the violent casting out of evil, but devoted to an affirmation of human wholeness and solidarity.

The Growing Stone carries the process to an even greater length, however. The profound solitude of the earlier characters meant not only their sense of separation from each other but also their feeling of alienation from the material world. Their moments of illumination involve an ephemeral intuition of oneness with the desert, with the cracking stones and with the wheeling stars. As we noted before, the setting of this last story is no longer an arid landscape, but rather a teeming jungle. As the title suggests, in this climate the very stones may come alive and start to grow. Suddenly there is a joining of the animate and inanimate. The movement that was imperceptible in the Saharan desert can be seen all around in the Brazilian rain forest.

In several of the other stories, water and the sea have appeared fleetingly as images of harmony between the human and the material universe. In Iguape, the flow is universal. D'Arrast first appears crossing a river, he awakens into a rain, and he has come to control the flow of yet another river. The sea too is close by, and the Cook worked on a ship. The plunge into the water, a motif we have seen in *The Fall* and *The Artist at Work*, is most fully realized in the Cook; but the statue of Jesus too swam in the sea, and D'Arrast plunges into a symbolic sea, the human tide of the procession. In the final moment, the river has become part of D'Arrast; he feels his joy as a flow within him. Thus *The Growing Stone* concludes the collection on a vision of almost total reconciliation. Not merely all people but all things and all people are somehow joined in a common feeling and a common purpose.

These happy images do not, however, supply answers to the philosophical questions at the base of Camus's thought. What takes place in Iguape is no permanent solution, even for D'Arrast and for his newfound friends. Eventually, they must part; the Frenchman will have to return to France, and the Iguapeans will go about their lives as before, although presumably without the regular floods. This, as we noted before, is a philosophical tale, which particularizes abstract ideas while it simplifies reality. Iguape is Camus's El Dorado, the home of an ideal community.

Candide returned from El Dorado of his own free will. The timeless uniformity of Voltaire's utopia was in fact boring, and Candide came to regret the very evil that had caused his expulsion from the paradise of Thunder-ten-tronckh, the differences of status among people. Candide wanted to go home and be richer than anyone else.

Camus's utopia has far more plausibility, and its fatal flaw is not in its structure but simply in the nature of things: it cannot last. It is a fortunate combination of circumstances and people ready to appreciate them. Such moments of shared joy are as much miracles as the stone or the statue of Iguape. It is as if they too wash up occasionally from the sea, along with the wreckage, the drownings, the floods. The lesson we should take from the story is to be prepared to seize the moment when it comes. D'Arrast contributes his part in creating the miracle of reconciliation, partly through the very practical actions that we have seen. The central gesture, however, defies rationality. In seizing the Cook's stone, D'Arrast perfectly illustrates the need to take the burden one finds at hand. Neither the vow he fulfills nor the load he bears is what he might have chosen, but our choices are never entirely free. The hope that Camus offers us is that by making the choices that do come our way, we may indeed overcome that solitude and despair by affirming our human solidarity.

As we remarked in the beginning of the chapter, *The Growing*

Stone seems anomalous in *Exile and the Kingdom* because of its loose structure, its profusion of characters, and its exotic setting. Furthermore, the ending seems strikingly more hopeful than in any of the first five stories. As the final story, it occupies a position of unusual importance in the collection, for it will largely determine the overall impression. To the degree that readers perceive unity and order, they must depend heavily on *The Growing Stone* to provide the sense of an ending, to make the diverse characters, events, and themes cohere. On closer examination, we will see that the apparent strangeness of this concluding story conceals many strong links to all the other stories—so many, in fact, that the optimism of the ending may require a retrospective rereading of the whole work.

To a remarkable extent, the main characters of all six stories are alike, and begin in like situations. All are middle-aged and feel themselves at a point of crisis. Their dreams have gone unfulfilled, their energies are waning, their hopes are gone. With Janine and Yvars, the detailed realization of their aging occupies much of the story. Of all the characters, the Renegade has most flatly failed; and he tries to murder his own past when he kills the new missionary, who might have succeeded where he had failed. With these three, recollections of their disappointments obsess them. Even Daru, who had apparently found his place in his little desert schoolhouse, is led by the arrival of the prisoner to recall his first days there and his early frustrations. Daru, however, has come to need the colorlessness, the solitude, the silence, just as Janine needs Marcel, Yvars his trade, and the Renegade his masters.

Since Jonas's whole career is told, he presents a slightly different case; the critical moment does not begin until quite late in the story, when his inspiration deserts him. No incident occurs, but a progressive paralysis of the will and a growing indifference to his work. A few key phrases bring out the analogy to the others, however: "for the first time, he was bothered by the people he kept bumping into everywhere" (146)[19] and "the cold pierced him to the marrow" (147).[20] Jonas's progressive breakdown leads, not to a single dramatic revelation, but to idleness, drink, and womanizing, until his wife's sorrow leads him to make one last effort; and his final painting is comparable to the visions of the other characters.

D'Arrast thinks less about his past than the others, and we learn relatively little about it. Outwardly, he seems happy and successful, but there are signs that he too has reached a point of crisis. In response to the Cook's questions, he reveals that he once made a promise, "in a shipwreck? —If you wish," and he goes on to say, "Someone was about to die through my fault. It seems to me that I called out.—Did you promise? —No. I should have liked to promise. —Long ago? —Not long before coming here." And finally: "I used to be proud; now I'm alone" (187).[21] Whatever one infers from this discreet confession, which makes D'Arrast sound a little like Jonas, Clamence, or Tarrou, it plainly implies a recent personal failure of some sort. Moreover, like Janine and the others, D'Arrast feels a vague longing, of which he grows most aware after seeing the stone of the title: "He too was waiting in front of the grotto under the same film of water, and he didn't know for what. He had been waiting constantly, to tell the truth, for a month since he had arrived in this country" (180).[22] D'Arrast's prestige and success as an engineer overlay a dissatisfaction comparable to all the others, expressed in terms that are in fact identical to Janine's.

The six central figures, differing widely in profession and class and intellect, nonetheless all share the trait of physical solidity. D'Arrast is called a colossus; Janine suffers from her large body; Jonas is tall and rugged. Yvars has dry, hard muscles like a vinestock, Daru is broad and powerful enough to break the Arab in half, and the Renegade has a hard, mulish head. To all of them, their bodies seem encumbrances. Janine and Yvars especially feel themselves stiffening and weakening. The Renegade has been tortured and mutilated. Jonas collapses from fatigue at the end of the story, after feeling increasingly cramped in his crowded apartment. Even Daru is bothered by the Arab's presence, and feels vulnerable. D'Arrast feels nauseated, suffers from a migraine, and almost collapses, despite his strength. The importance of their solid bodies is emphasized by the regular contrasts to the other characters. D'Arrast dominates everyone else, especially the short, fat Cook and the small, thin Socrates.

Camus shows no concern for a psychological or sociological analysis of these characters. He makes no effort to sentimentalize their plights, and even less to generalize about the social conditions. Daru and D'Arrast have virtually no past. The factors that have affected the other characters' lives—the war that ruined Marcel's business, the Renegade's peasant origins, Jonas's broken home—are not perceived by the characters themselves as determinant. In every case, the central event concerns a person who must confront his or her own limitations, whether personal, physical, or professional. They have slightly different substance in each story, but in each there is a moment of failure and loss, which gains plausibility from the fact that it corresponds to a well-documented moment of crisis in the average person's life; but Camus always stresses the moral and philosophical implications, never the social or historical causes. The limits encountered by all the characters are, in the final analysis, those of human mortality and human existence in the absurd universe. Janine is most explicit about the underlying source of her anxiety: "She too was afraid of death" (29).[23] As the first story of the collection, *The Adulterous Woman* serves as a kind of preface and suggests that the nameless anxiety that comes to all the central figures springs from a similar origin. The bodies, originally strong and healthy, bring the first warnings of the impending crisis. These characters's vigor, at an earlier date, was a delusion of possibilities, an appearance of superiority to the common fate that allowed them to be indifferent to their place. Their European origins, in the context of Algerian and Brazilian settings, reinforce this notion. Although in various ways they all admit to having held this illusion of infinite capacity or eternal youth, Jonas most concretely expresses the idea in his "star," as if the universe were watching over him. Ultimately, though, reality demands the same price from him as from everyone else, whether he recognizes it or not. He too has to agonize; he too has to sacrifice; he too has to drive his body to the limits of endurance, as D'Arrast most dramatically does in the final pages of the book, carrying the stone.

While the body provides one form of warning, the settings of the stories consistently provide another. At the start of each one, the central character is isolated, spiritually if not physically. For Jonas and d'Arrast, the realization of their solitude comes to them well into the story. But D'Arrast's triumph over isolation is all the more impressive because he is so strikingly alone and out of place. Along with the sense of loneliness, Camus creates an atmosphere of disorientation. The long introductory section of *The Growing Stone*, where D'Arrast travels through night and mist, drifting in and out of sleep, waking into dreamlike scenes such as the Japanese settlement, serves in part to recapitulate similar scenes in the other stories—Janine riding through the sandstorm, Yvars and the Renegade in the blinding light, Daru looking at a landscape made featureless by snow, and Jonas sitting long hours in the dark.

Camus constructs his stories so as to emphasize the strangeness of the familiar. As the characters look about them, their habitual settings seem altered and well-known objects unrecognizable. The discomfort they feel in their bodies extends to all the material world. For D'Arrast, as for Janine, a journey into foreign territory provides the initial shock; but with all the characters, the sense of growing separation from the physical world is meant to translate for us the awareness of a radical alienation, the awakening of a rational mind in a meaningless universe of things.

Having set each of the stories in motion with a similar structure, Camus proceeds by means of a number of repeated motifs and themes. By motif, I mean simply a specific object or situation that recurs; by theme, an idea that is explicitly mentioned. Many of these are familiar, not only in these stories, but also in Camus's other works. Many critics have looked for the works's coherence in the themes of exile and the kingdom, for example, or of solidarity and fraternity, or the motifs of the natural environment, sun, sea, desert, and so on.

For Camus, stone is the fundamental image of the concrete universe, and appears in many forms. The mystical stones of the final story, *The Growing Stone*, point to the positive symbolism; the stone is humanity's burden of responsibility, akin to Sisyphus's stone. The growing stone of the grotto, consecrated by superstition, nonetheless represents the fruitful cooperation of people and their environment. D'Arrast, one of those (like Dr. Rieux) who fight against creation as they found it by building roads and dikes, may at the same time learn from the humble acceptance he observes among these poor Brazilians. The struggle to dominate nature can never be won; even the stones may grow again. The other stone, which D'Arrast carries to fulfill the Cook's vow, shows human solidarity at its finest, in the struggle with the world. D'Arrast bears it to the Cook's hut rather than to the church, for his faith is in people, not gods. Inside the hut, it occupies the central place, in the middle of the human circle, like a kind of altar to humanity.

As we have seen, stone was important in all the other stories except *The Artist at Work*; but once again, it is the first story, *The Adulterous Woman*, to which the concluding story seems most fitting as a response. For Janine, stone represented not only the harsh real world around her but also something spiritual, linked to the Mosaic law. In her climactic swoon, she discovers a oneness with the universe, stars and stones alike. D'Arrast actually becomes part of this universe.[24] Like the miraculous statue, he "bucks the human tide" (206)[25] to come to the Cook's aid; like the miraculous stone, he grows "taller and more massive each time he came back to life" (161)[26] in the beginning, then "straightening up until he was suddenly enormous" (212)[27] at the end. The waters of the river, whose sound fills him with "a tumultuous happiness," also flow within him as a "surge of obscure and panting joy" (212),[28] just as the water of the night had filled Janine.

Most of the characters have not understood their place in the material universe at the start, if they ever do. They learn from a new experience of pain, but also by reaching a point from which to take a broader view. At the same time, this perspective may suggest a feeling of superiority to the world and to others, which must be overcome or surrendered before peace can be felt. All the characters grow aware of their feelings on elevations— Janine on her parapet, Daru on his hill, Jonas in his loft, and D'Arrast on the balcony.

If revelation occurs on the heights, however, the hero must come back down to profit from the experience. Again, D'Arrast illustrates the most positive instance of this descent; on the balcony with the town notables, he awaits the procession, but leaves instantly when the Cook does not appear with the others. Down among the people, he first tries to revive the Cook, then takes up the stone himself. The analogies both of action and of language between Janine and D'Arrast are unmistakable; retrospectively, Janine's return to her husband may be regarded as a necessary resumption of her human responsibilities.[29] Daru and Yvars remain on their elevations at the end of their stories, not necessarily punished, but still unable to integrate their own happiness and the conditions of their lives. The Renegade and Jonas are brought down, the one by force, the other by exhaustion, and therefore with quite opposite expectations. Both were wrong, however—the Renegade to suppose that he could serve a god, Jonas to suppose that a god (his star) existed to serve him. The Renegade must learn the truth in the most brutal fashion, getting a mouthful of salt when he was aching with thirst. Jonas, on the other hand, in painting the ambiguous solidary/solitary canvas, seems to be on the road to a productive compromise, especially since he has reaffirmed his love of his family and the beauty of the noises of humanity without abandoning his art. Still, like his Old Testament namesake, he had to learn love as well as courage.

One of the most common episodes in Camus's stories, as we saw in *The Silent Men*, is a meal or a drink. Part of a long heritage of symbolism, the act of consuming links people with the material world on the one hand, and with the divinity, through Communion, on the other. Shared meals have a complex ritual, itself full of meanings to those who understand it. D'Arrast illustrates the full possibilities of the communal meal. Significantly, his friend among the Brazilians is a ship's cook, whose work is to prepare the nourishment of others. D'Arrast shares several drinks of hospitality, and several official dinners; but the most important is the dinner of black beans the Cook makes specially for D'Arrast. At the end of the story, when D'Arrast has borne the stone to the Cook's hut, the circle re-forms around the hearth, and D'Arrast is welcomed to his place. The collection thus ends on a note of harmony and brotherhood.

The Growing Stone contains a great deal of dialog compared with the earlier stories of the book. In fact, the first three stories treat silence and the inability to communicate as a major theme. In *The Guest*, although Daru can speak Arabic, yet his conversation with his guest goes continually awry. In the end, Daru's refusal to listen may have cost him his kingdom.

Both Jonas and D'Arrast, creative and professional men of the upper class and of Western Europe, escape the kind of muteness that afflicted the earlier characters. Jonas comes to suffer an artist's block, equivalent to a silence; as an artist, though, he takes on the responsibility for breaking through it. D'Arrast never seems troubled by lack of words; he responds forthrightly to the Cook's questions about his own background, about social conditions in France, and about his promise. Several times, Camus notes a hesitation on his part and on the Cook's part; but always the speaker goes ahead. D'Arrast is fortunate that his hosts, although Portuguese is their native language, chatter willingly in bad French or Spanish; but D'Arrast also speaks more than one language. D'Arrast's greatest linguistic accomplishment is to have found the words with which to judge the Police Chief; the rhetoric does no more than make acceptable to the others what D'Arrast had been saying all along. In reality, he avoids judging and punishing the Police Chief. Yet it is precisely the mark of D'Arrast's heroism that he accepts the challenge of communication at all levels. It was not sufficient for him to be morally right; he had to be so within a social context. His flattering speech is the sort of formula that Daru could not find for Balducci.

Language is, then, a key factor in Camus's moral vision. The early stories show that silence is not necessarily a "sin" or even a sign of dullness; many of the characters understand the truth of the human condition without being able to act upon it. The action alone may be a great achievement—the greater if the inarticulate hero goes unsung. Those who would fully realize Camus's ideal must assume a further burden, however, that of the writer himself, to convey something of that knowledge to others. Only by sharing experiences and the fruits of experience can human beings achieve solidarity among themselves. This is what D'Arrast achieves in many different areas, most of them already familiar to us from the other stories.

The six stories have in common not only themes and motif but also a general plot structure. Near the beginning, a character expresses or remembers hopes and expectations that have been disappointed. Then a change of some sort takes place, so that the disappointed character finds a new perspective on the events. By the end, a subtle reversal has occurred, and the original position is transformed into its opposite. The change may not be for the better, at least at the practical level; Daru rediscovers solitude, and the Renegade dies. Moreover, the change usually has little emotional impact on the reader, and frequently leaves us wondering what has actually happened. There are no melodramatic reunions, no heart-rending separations, no poetic justice, and no tragic mistakes.

With D'Arrast, the change is complex, but it produces hope. D'Arrast comes to Iguape as a prestigious outsider, to whom even the highest local officials defer; yet in the final scene, he waits to be invited to sit among the poorest folk of the town. A religious skeptic, he has fulfilled a pious, even superstitious, vow. He has calmly tolerated abuse from the Chief of Police and exclusion from the Negroes' dancing. But the rewards for these reversals are similar, more positive changes: the foreigner has found a kind of home, the lonely man has found friends, the exile has found a kingdom. When D'Arrast arrived, he brought not only his authority as an engineer and plans for construction but also a nameless longing and a recent personal failure. For once, the revelation comes to a person ready to accept it, the opportunity is seized; and if our final view of D'Arrast is a strange one, it is nonetheless hard to see how it can be anything but hopeful. But what has happened to D'Arrast is enough like what happened to Janine, to Yvars, to Daru, to Jonas, and even to the Renegade, that his small victory must imply theirs, too.

The reason for the lack of high drama in the plots is that the changes happen within. Even where a striking event occurs, such as the Renegade's murder or Lassalle's daughter's seizure, the external conditions are not altered so much as the central figure's awareness and understanding of them. The stories show people confronting the realization that things are not what they seem. The underlying purpose, of course, is to force the reader into the same situation; and so each story also induces an expectation on the reader's part that proves false. There is a transaction between author and reader that parallels the one described in the text.

In several cases, the very title sets up a false expectation or prepares an ironic misunderstanding. The Adulterous Woman commits no adultery; The Artist at Work ceases to work; the Silent Men include finally the boss as well as the men; The Guest—l'hôte—may be host or guest, Daru or the Arab, either in either role. Often the apparent action turns out to be secondary as well; Janine has no affair with the jackal-soldier; the workmen do not confront the boss; the prisoner never challenges Daru; even the Renegade's murder of the new missionary matters less than his sudden reconversion to a religion of mercy.

The Growing Stone is yet another misleading title, for the miraculous growing stone is not the most important stone, the one carried by the Cook and D'Arrast. In some sense, however, the title informs the whole story; metaphorically, the two stones are the same, and represent the material world successfully invested with human meanings. The stone they carry grows in a metaphorical sense too, as its weight becomes more and more painful and harder to bear. In the context of *Exile and the Kingdom*, the stone D'Arrast seizes and carries is a reply to the stone Daru flings away; the stone that grows is a contrast to the stones Janine hears cracking into dust. Because the story does not fulfill the immediate implications of its title, we must look for broader symbolic meanings.

In the haphazard development of the plot, *The Growing Stone* resembles some of the other stories as well. The relationship between D'Arrast and Socrates, so important at the beginning, turns out to be incidental, like Janine's with the jackal-soldier. D'Arrast's hostile encounter with the Police Chief has no repercussions, like Daru's conflict with Balducci. The construction of the dike raises no dramatic issues, just as the strikers' return to work leads to no confrontation in *The Silent Men*. *The Growing Stone* brings together an exceptionally large number of these false leads, potential actions that never take place; but it is merely echoing a technique Camus uses throughout. It is, in fact, only our readers' awareness of literary conventions that leads us to see possible plots in every detail or incident. Our belief in literary meaning resembles the faith of the Iguapeans in the Growing Stone: phenomena cannot be accidental when they appear so clearly to signify something.

D'Arrast, however, remains uncommitted in his beliefs; Camus gives us only his actions as clues to his mind. It is significant that in his climactic gesture, even D'Arrast is portrayed as unaware of his motives: he leaves the balcony "quick as lightning, without excusing himself" (206),[30] pushes through the crowd in an "impetuous way" (206),[31] finds himself beside the Cook "without knowing how" (207),[32] takes the stone "suddenly" (209),[33] and changes course, bypassing the church and heading for the hut, "without knowing why" (210).[34] D'Arrast possesses from the start a strong sense of brotherhood with people and of unity with the universe, which Janine glimpses momentarily in her dash to the parapet, a gesture very much like D'Arrasts's. Even D'Arrast, however, must allow his instinctive fraternal love to direct his actions. His spontaneity, his tolerance, his freedom are partly learned from the people of Iguape, especially the Cook.

The only strong desire D'Arrast expresses during the story is to visit the poor section of the town. The traditional form of plot, where the hero's will encounters obstacles until it imposes itself or is defeated, is present only in this area. D'Arrast seems to want to be accepted among these people. More than he wants to build the dike, more than he wants to conciliate the notables, he wants to know the lives of Socrates, the Cook, the old man, the dark girl, the pilgrims, the faithful. Besides the conventional virtues of the poor—openness, directness, simplicity, and so on—the Cook gives D'Arrast an important insight into his faith and his sense of place within the universe. To D'Arrast's skeptical question, "Has the good Jesus always answered you?" the Cook replies, "Always. ... no, Captain!" D'Arrast triumphs: "Well, then?" But the Cook only laughs and responds, "Well, he's free, isn't he?" (187).[35] The Cook's relationship to reality is a fraternal one, built on an affectionate respect for the Other's freedom—in this case, the freedom of the entire external universe personified as Jesus. It is immediately after this conversation that D'Arrast finds the solution to the problem of the Police Chief, a solution that respects not only D'Arrast's principles and the Chief's freedom, but also the faith of the Judge and other notables in their system of order.

1. P. 1660: "éternuements cataclysmiques."

2. P. 1669: "D'Arrast se sentit vaguement agacé."

3. P. 1675: "Sans bienveillance, comme s'il parlait à un étranger"; "ils ne veulent pas que tu restes maintenant."

4. P. 1664: "sur un ton impératif."

5. P. 1671: "pût commencer dans un climat de concorde et d'amitié."

6. This incident, like many others in this story, is modeled closely on an experience Camus relates in the notebooks he kept during a journey to Brazil in 1949; Quilliot reprints the relevant passages in the notes, pp. 2063-74, the account of the rude policeman being on p. 2072. The true version gives little clue to what significance Camus attached to it at the time; he relates it rather ironically. And, of course, it tells us nothing about his reasons for retaining it later for the story or about the way it functions in the story for the reader.

7. The penitent carrying the stone is also taken from reality, but in this case with a radical change: in the actual event, the man fulfilled his vow unaided (pp. 2073-74).

8. The indirect source of this detail is Camus's observation that his Brazilian driver looked like Auguste Comte (p. 2069).

9. P. 1672: "un superbe chromo où Saint Georges, avec des airs séducteurs, prenait avantage d'un dragon moustachu." The print of Saint George and most of the details of the ceremony are taken from Camus's impressions of a *macumba* in Brazil (pp. 2063-67).

10. P. 1672: "représentant un dieu cornu. Il brandissait, la mine farouche, un couteau démesuré, en papier d'argent."

11. P. 1675: "un arc vert et jaune, muni de sa flèche, au bout de laquelle était embroché un oiseau multicolore."

12. P. 1675: "un étrange cri d'oiseau."

13. P. 1674: "remuant de droite à gauche sa face animale, aboyait sans arrêt."

14. P. 173: "possédé."

15. P. 1673: "le champ de bataille du dieu."

16. P. 1672: "Décroise les bras . . . Tu te serres, tu empêches l'esprit du saint de descendre."

17. P. 1672: "dieu bestial."

18. Once again this attitude is based on Camus's own; he had been asked to unfold his arms, and obeyed docilely (p. 2065). His opinion of the ceremony as a whole, at least as the notebooks record it, was succinct and rather contemptuous: "I like the night and the sky, more than the gods of men"—"J'aime la nuit et le ciel, plus que les dieux des hommes" (p. 2067). D'Arrast's seizing the stone thus exposes a fantasy of intervention and involvement that Camus did not acknowledge at the time.

19. P. 1646: "pour la première fois, il était gêné par les gens qu'il rencontrait partout."

20. P. 1646: "le froid pénétrait jusqu'à son coeur."

21. P. 1670: "Dans un naufrage? —Si tu veux . . . Quelqu'un allait mourir par ma faute. Il me semble que j'ai appelé. —Tu as promis? —Non. J'aurais voulu promettre. — Il y a longtemps? —Peu avant de venir ici. . . . J'étais fier, maintenant je suis seul."

22. P. 1666: "Lui aussi attendait, devant cette grotte, sous la même brume d'eau, et il ne savait quoi. Il ne cessait d'attendre, en vérité, depuis un mois qu'il était arrivé dans ce pays."

23. P. 1570: "elle aussi avait peur de mourir."

24. I am indebted to two excellent articles for some of the ideas in this paragraph, and elsewhere in this chapter: Thomas Claire, "Landscape and Religious Imagery in Camus's 'La Pierre qui pousse,'" and Michael Issacharoff, "Une Symbolique de l'espace: Lecture de 'La Pierre qui pousse' d'Albert Camus."

25. P. 1680: "remontant la marée humaine."

26. P. 1656: "plus grand et plus massif à chaque résurrection."

27. P. 1683: "redressant toute sa taille, énorme soudain."

28. Pp. 1683–84: "un bonheur tumultueux . . . le flot d'une joie obscure et haletante." The English translation does not fully convey the way in which the first sentence ("il écouta monter en lui le flot d'une joie obscure et haletante") is echoed in the second: "Seule, la rumeur du fleuve montait jusqu'à eux à travers l'air lourd. D'Arrast, debout dans l'ombre, écoutait, sans rien voir, et le bruit des eaux l'emplissait d'un bonheur tumultueux."

29. It was disappointing to my students of the late 1970s that Camus seemed to assume *ma*ternity and solidarity for women, *fra*ternity and solidarity for men. The latter has much greater scope and is trammeled by fewer social exigencies. Maternity, as Camus is using it here, is as metaphorical as adultery, and is self-defined. Janine transforms actual motherhood, which she has not experienced, into a generalized sense of responsibility for an Other, and then accepts Marcel as that Other. For all Camus's heroes, virtually all of them male, that appears to be the right moral choice: one must seize the burden at hand. But for the Renegade, it would have been a humble parish in France; for Yvars, his boss; for Daru, the Arab prisoner; for D'Arrast, the Cook. For Jonas, it would include Louise and his children, but also his painting. For women, somehow the burden at hand always turns out to be a husband or a child. I think Camus anticipated many points of a feminist analysis in his presentation of Janine's situation, and there is much interest in his exploration—limited though it is—of the implications of his moral thought for women.

Most of the time, however, like his contemporaries Saint-Exupéry and Malraux, he evades the problem by contriving to write about almost all-male societies. You could almost end up believing that women were immune to bubonic plague. For some interesting comments on Camus's misogyny, and his treatment of women in his earlier works, see Anthony Rizzuto, *Camus' Imperial Vision*, especially pp. 78 and 127.

30. P. 1680: "D'un seul mouvement, sans s'excuser."

31. P. 1680: "d'un mouvement emporté."

32. P. 1681: "sans qu'il sût comment."

33. P. 1682: "Soudain."

34. P. 1682: "sans savoir pourquoi."

35. P. 1670: "Ton bon Jésus t'a toujours répondu?—Toujours, non, Capitaine! —Alors? —Eh bien, il est libre, non?"

 Eight

Camus's Last Words

Perhaps it is redundant ever to say that a death is premature, and Camus more than anyone would have protested against the idea of a timely death. Certainly, though, the accident that cut short Camus's life stunned the public more than is normal, and even now renews our sense of tragic irony in human existence. Because of this accident, *Exile and the Kingdom* represents Camus's final statement; and interesting though it is, by its very nature this collection of stories seems less a climactic final summary than a set of tentative clues, composed and conceived moreover during a period of several years. With Camus, this inconclusiveness is all the more tantalizing because he was quite clearly evolving rapidly in the late 1950s. In the personal sphere, the adulation of Camus's admirers had made his public image almost as unbearable to him as the hostility of his enemies— some of them former friends. On the historical plane, the heroic age of revolt in the Resistance had given way to a postwar era of political pettiness at home, apparently insoluble conflicts in Algeria, and a cold-war sense of doom.

The Fall, originally intended to be part of *Exile and the Kingdom* but written in a kind of inspired outburst and published separately in 1956, reveals the process of self-examination Camus was going through. In a brilliant article written in 1963,[1] René Girard demonstrated that *The Fall* retried "the stranger," who had been the hero of Camus's first novel and the spokesman for a generation in the 1940s. In Girard's view, *The Fall* does not repudiate but rather transcends *The Stranger*, and is a far greater work, one deserving to rank with the fiction of Cervantes, Balzac, Dickens, and Dostoevski. Clamence, whose kinship to the artist Jonas we have already seen, partly represents Camus, the "generous lawyer" who defended Meursault; but Clamence has undergone the devastating realization that there was never a difference between the innocent criminal, the evil judge, and the generous lawyer.

Girard is perhaps too severe in denouncing *The Stranger*, although a corrective was surely in order, for Meursault had become a kind of cult hero. Moreover, Camus had done himself a disservice by adding a preface to an American edition of *L'Etranger*[2] in which he says that Meursault "is condemned because he does not play the game" and "refuses to lie,"[3] and alleges that "in our society a man who does not cry at the funeral of his mother is likely to be sentenced to death."[4] Moreover, Meursault is a Christ-figure, "the only Christ we deserve."[5] Some of these claims are patent exaggerations—Meursault does play certain games and does lie upon occasion—and others were uttered "paradoxically"[6] in Camus's own term, that is, simply as provocative sallies that have long been a staple of French intellectual repartie. Hostile critics have seized on this preface, however, to justify an exact identification of Meursault's point of view with Camus's. Even a defender like Philip Thody feels that Camus has thereby endorsed Meursault's racism.[7] Yet we know that an author may not be his own best critic, and ordinarily, a pure first-person narrator like Meursault would be understood as separate from his creator. In Camus's lifetime, those who wished to attack the man, the moralist, or the political activist could legitimately confuse the author and his creation, and cite what evidence they chose; but now, surely, *The Stranger* has the right to be judged as a work of fiction, with a certain autonomy.

There have, of course, been favorable reconsiderations as well, especially Brian Fitch's *L'Etranger d'Albert Camus* (1972),[8] which analyzes the work from many different perspectives, and Jules Brody's luminous "Camus et la pensée tragique: *L'Etranger*."[9] It is important at least to recognize that the Meursault of the last pages is no longer the same person as the one described in the beginning. The murder, the trial, the prison, and the confrontation with the chaplain have given him new insight and moral understanding, which Brody persuasively compares to Oedipus's final illumination. The Meursault of part one is undeniably a petit bourgeois bureaucrat, a macho racist, and a callous murderer; if Camus wants us to admire him, it is obviously for none of those traits, but for the potential tragic hero within him.

Girard was nonetheless correct in calling attention to the childishly romantic pride and self-pity of Meursault's presentation of himself, which had seduced many readers. "We do not understand the disturbing role which violence plays in [*L'Etranger*]," says Girard, "probably because the novel is the latest successful formulation of the myth of the romantic self" (p. 527). The heroism Camus claimed for Meursault in his preface, many critics and readers had already accepted, with few reservations. To explain the flaw in *The Stranger*, Girard supposes that Camus began with an a priori principle and invented facts to fit it. The principle itself, moreover, arose largely from the writer's own sense of himself. The pose of indifference, the concealed longing for recognition, the devious provocations, all these characterize the not-yet-successful young writer. All are exposed, demystified, denounced in *The Fall*.

Without denying that Camus projected an immature version of himself onto Meursault, yet I would allow him a nobler inspiration too. In a famous scene in *The Stranger*, Meursault notices a journalist in the courtroom who seems to have a look different from the others, and Meursault says, "I had a strange impression of being looked at by myself."[10] This reporter is an admitted figure for the author, who did in fact cover trials in Algiers, and who must have seen many criminals as innocently unaware of their responsibility as Meursault. In other words, Camus devised his principle to account for an observed fact, which remains, however, inexplicable: a man to all outward appearances normal may commit a monstrous crime and feel nothing; or perhaps one should say, may feel nothing and commit a monstrous crime. By adopting his point of view, Camus romanticized him, so seductively that millions of readers believed in him and identified with him. By the time he wrote *The Fall*, Camus recognized the inadequacy of his presentation in *The Stranger*, in part perhaps because he had outgrown his youthful romanticism. When he returns to the problem in *The Fall*, however, it is not only because he wants to correct an earlier mistake but also because the "innocent murderer" still haunts his conscience.

The effort to transcend *The Stranger* is visible throughout *Exile and the Kingdom* as well as in *The Fall*. Several of the stories approximate the narrative structure of *The Stranger*. An ordinary person in ordinary circumstances is somehow drawn into an encounter with the absurd. The central figures, like Meursault, lurk in the margins of society; they say little and do little. At least until the story begins, they appear to have reflected very little on their own lives; they are, like Meursault, sleepwalkers, going through the motions of life but unconscious. The stories tell of a moment when each of these characters awakens, if only momentarily, often as a result of some unforeseen disturbance. The disturbance in Meursault's case was, of course, the murder that Girard singles out as the locus of the flaw, explainable neither as willed, nor fated, nor purely accidental. In *Exile and the Kingdom*, the disturbances are far less dramatic and more plausible, and the pertinence of the moral analysis is correspondingly greater. In *The Adulterous Woman*, as we saw, Janine's crime is purely symbolic, and the trial only implied; nonetheless, critics have willingly pronounced judgment, just as Camus realized he himself had done in *The Stranger*. So too Yvars, Daru, Jonas, and D'Arrast: to the extent that each one offends, it is through passivity, not willful malice; but their world is not so full of snares as to make murderers of them unawares.

In *Exile and the Kingdom*, only *The Renegade* does not conform to that pattern. The Renegade is, in fact, the precise opposite of Meursault and the others, anything but an ordinary, diffident person; he is a proselytizer, a bearer of the Word. He is no sleeper—indeed, he watches through the night; and he has thought about his condition, albeit wrongly. His murder of the missionary is premeditated; indeed, the story is the text of his premeditation. Even the Renegade, however, may come to resemble Meursault in his final moments, if we take his last hallucinatory appeal for mercy as the same sort of death's-door revelation as Meursault's wish for a large hostile audience at his execution.

The first-person narration also links *The Renegade* to *The Stranger*. In the earlier novel, the ethical paradox of the innocent murderer is doubled by an aesthetic paradox. For the novel to exist at all, the silent, unreflective hero must be transformed into a garrulous and perceptive monologist, who delivers his discourse without motive and without audience. As we have seen, this is one of the significant features of *The Renegade*; the sullen, incomprehensible criminal on the verge of death can speak to us only through fiction. The disembodied voice is itself a form of alienation.

The number of motifs that Camus used throughout his life, from *The Stranger* to *Exile and the Kingdom*, is very large; the sun, the sea, silence, and food are some of the more obvious that we have considered in the stories. They serve, of course, to situate and particularize the themes that obsessed Camus. *Exile and the Kingdom* was not conceived as a theoretical statement, the counterpart to *The Myth of Sisyphus* and *The Rebel*. It does, however, illustrate the maturing of Camus's thought, especially on some of the practical consequences of his ideas, or on the difficulty of translating ideas into behavior.

The Stranger is an effort to reconstruct a personality. It is no doubt a fragmented psyche, as many critics have observed. From the paratactic syntax to the narrator's frequent confessions that events made no sense, the portrait accepts its own incoherence. For all that, it coheres, if only because the "I" remembers itself. But this is a fictional "I," a thoughtful mind projected into a purely sensual being. The author, as Girard rightly saw and as Camus acknowledges in *The Fall*, is doing precisely the same thing as the defense attorney, the examining magistrate, the prosecutor, the judges, the jurors, and the chaplain. Each one offers a portrait of Meursault that attempts to make sense of him. And in many cases, Meursault has only to say yes or no in order to impose an interpretation on the world.

Since none of the portraits is accurate, however, Meursault experiences each offer as an effort to force a hypocritical mask upon him. He therefore maintains a stubborn silence, leaving the jury to select the most plausible of the portraits—except that Camus has put words into his mouth and transferred the case before a new jury of readers. Meursault has no chance to deny this version, even though he had protested in advance against such a procedure, remarking that the trial was going on without him. The novelist evades the objection, however, by appearing to join in it, by giving us the illusion as we read of sharing Meursault's feelings.

The Fall reveals Camus's misgivings about that procedure, his suspicions about his own motives, and his recognition that murderers are never innocent. To make Meursault a mere martyr to sincerity is, moreover, to oversimplify him worse than even the simpleminded judges, lawyers, and chaplains had done. Human nature remains problematic, however, and *Exile and the Kingdom* pursues the analysis without arriving at such pat answers. Both Janine and Yvars are mutes like Meursault, to whom Camus lends perception and articulateness. Both are, in most respects, more victims than villains. Janine is guilty of little more than a fleeting sense of discontent, Yvars fails to express a sympathy he actually feels. To the outside observer, the woman who leaves her husband's bed at night may seem to commit a serious betrayal, and the workers who refuse a word of condolence to the stricken father seem to create a pointless enmity. These are not innocent murderers but innocent sinners. Yet they are sinners.

What seems to have complicated Camus's view of the ordinary person is the knowledge that perfect detachment of any sort is impossible. Tarrou, in *The Plague*, had demonstrated the principle in highly dramatic fashion; but the characters of *The Plague* are for the most part educated and articulate. Many of them are writers of some kind, even Joseph Grand, who transforms the dreary bureaucrat into a hero of commitment. And as many have pointed out before, the plague is both inhuman and unmistakably evil; the responsibility thrust upon the people of Oran is unambiguous. For Janine and Yvars, that is not so. They are leading the most normal of lives, minding their own business, trying to do no harm; the test comes upon them without warning, and in a guise unrecognizably simple, it demands of them something they cannot do. Camus is still playing the generous lawyer when he writes such stories; but he is no longer so certain of his case, and no longer so determined to win. He is content to strive for fidelity to the truth of human nature and reality, and to base his plea on the hope that we will recognize our common humanity.

The Guest most closely resembles *The Stranger* in its content, for in both stories there is a silent murderer who seems to collaborate in his own conviction and punishment. One of the signs of Camus's new outlook is his humanization of the judges, among them Daru; but before he is a judge, Daru is one of the group of common folk like Janine and Yvars, trying to do his job, trying to do no harm, finding crisis thrust upon him. Daru does more than just avoid doing harm; he is certainly a force for good in the world in the usual sense. He brings education and material aid to people in need; in brotherhood, he shares their poverty. It is impossible, in my opinion, to claim that he shares Clamence's secret guilt; that is, to accuse Daru of doing good for ego gratification, of being alone and poor so as to be seen and admired. He did not seek this job, but originally would have preferred to be elsewhere. He has accepted his place and made the best of it, coming to love it in the process. Yet just like the others, guilt seeks him out and attaches itself to him. Janine, Yvars, and Daru all realize what I think Camus was attempting in Meursault: a lonely, humble figure, unjustly condemned by a justice in which we readers and Camus largely concur. These are subtler works than *The Stranger*; the characters are fuller, more human, more familiar. The incidents in which they incur guilt are less dramatic but more plausible, more typical and hence seem more inevitable. The procedures of justice have been abstracted; implicit in the forms and in the language, judgment takes shape in the reader's mind, where we can neither deny its inevitability, nor remedy its injustice, nor escape our own complicity.

For in the end, Camus seems to have thought that judgment

was an unavoidable human activity. The professional judges of *The Stranger* and *The Plague* are two-dimensional caricatures, observed from the immense distance of Meursault's incomprehension and Rieux's dislike. Clamence, the judge-penitent, is a sudden closeup of those same judges, now vividly real and surprisingly like Camus himself, and like us readers too. Such self-righteous judges deserve to be exposed. Camus never came to think of judging as an easy task or one that any person should want to do. Judges are, however, only human beings, no different from common people and common criminals.

Daru becomes a victim because the role of judge is forced on him. The Arab prisoner who passes into his care resembles Meursault in many respects. Sullen and mute, he gives Daru no clue on which to base an understanding of his crime or of his character. Daru asks him some of the very questions Meursault was asked, notably, whether he felt any regret. Where Meursault denied feeling regret and, to the reader if not to the judge, explained his inability to regret anything, the Arab communicates the same lack of feeling with an open-mouthed stare of incomprehension. As with Meursault, one can easily imagine judicial defenses for the Arab that range from self-defense to temporary insanity; he simply refuses to cooperate in any of them and lets the fact of his crime stand uncontested. Even more than Meursault, he seems indifferent to his own fate, passing up chances to escape and taking the road toward the prison at the end.

The Arab makes a better "stranger" than Meursault in many respects. He will be tried under a system of justice that is genuinely alien to him, whatever his real motives and intelligence may be. The possibility of his being convicted less for the crime than merely for being an Arab is all too plausible. Clearly, though, the social and political aspects so overdetermine the situation that the moral or philosophical point made in *The Stranger* would be totally lost. And so this stranger is never called on to explain himself to us, but is presented solely from the point of view of a judge, Daru, who is a peculiarly sympathetic and humane judge, but a judge all the same.

In the end, of course, Daru is judged himself—unfairly by the terms of most readers, but not all, and obviously not from the perspective of the mysterious "brothers." Daru makes a kind of amends to the savagely portrayed judges of the earlier works; he is as conscientious as they were perfunctory, as tolerant as they were rigid, as reluctant as they were eager, and it makes no difference to the outcome. Furthermore, he has been simultaneously judge and accused. In fact, perhaps his worst failing has been his refusal to judge, his willingness to free a murderer instead of assuming his part of humanity's responsibility to assert a moral order.

Such seems to be the implication of the final story in the collection, *The Growing Stone*. D'Arrast, a man much like Daru in his unpretentious generosity, finds himself obliged to dispense justice to a boorish policeman. Like Daru, he tries not to make a judgment, but the townspeople insist. As we have already seen, one of the signs of D'Arrast's victory is his success in finding a formula by which his own sense of detachment can be preserved and the town's need for a decisive verdict respected. Camus, through D'Arrast, seems to be acknowledging his respect for human justice. In this case, it serves to forge bonds of brotherhood and mutual good will. Even in its blunders and cruelties, it represents an effort toward a common defense against real evils. When Meursault acquiesces in his own execution and wishes for the crowd to greet him with cries of hate, at least in part he is recognizing the validity of the verdict. The court that convicted him did the right thing, even if for the wrong reason. No other institution and no mere persuasion could have awakened Meursault to the moral condition of humanity.

The judicial system in *The Stranger* works in constant collaboration with the church. In the first interrogation, the magistrate thrusts a crucifix into Meursault's face, and tries repeatedly to extort a confession of faith from him. In the final chapter, a still more persistent chaplain intrudes upon his last hours and provokes the cathartic outburst of rage. The questions that preoccupied Camus are religious questions; inevitably, a meditation on the meaning of existence, on moral responsibility, on death, must respond to a religious world view, if only implicitly. Camus's early response is obviously an angry denunciation, not only in *The Stranger* but also in *The Plague*, where Father Paneloux appears as one of the allies of the evil. When the harrowing death of Judge Othon's son breaches Paneloux's faith, he soon dies himself, as if he were incapable of surviving in the compromised universe of Rieux, Grand, and their colleagues.

Camus never changed his opinion of the organized church and the dogmatic believer. The Renegade reincarnates the all-or-nothing spirit of Paneloux, and in the encounter with absolute cruelty, he converts to worship of the evil fetish. When the rumor of a new missionary threatens to bring some moderating charity into the city of salt, the Renegade prevents it at the price of his own life. As with Paneloux, as with Meursault's chaplain, if Camus allows him a moment of grace, it is precisely in the moment of doubt.

Both *The Fall* and *Exile and the Kingdom* reveal a new attitude toward the Judeo-Christian interpretation of the "human condition."[11] The very titles, drawing on a fund of religious imagery, suggest the change. *The Fall* alludes constantly to Judeo-Christian mythology, in the hero's name, in the baptismal plunge into the water, in the infernal rings of Amsterdam, to cite only some of the most obvious. In *Exile and the Kingdom*, only *The Silent Men* lacks some direct link to a religious tradition. We have examined most of these already— the parable of the adulterous woman, the central character of *The Renegade*, the Book of Jonah, the miracle of the growing stone. *The Guest* was originally called *Cain*, and a recent article has explored the ways in which Camus drew on the Genesis story.[12]

This is certainly not to suggest that Camus had converted, or was even evolving in that direction. *The Renegade* proves otherwise. It does indicate that he was finding the treatments of the problems he had always been concerned with richer and more rewarding in religious writings than he had previously thought. In his earlier works, he turns naturally to classical antiquity for symbols congenial to his ideas. Sisyphus and Caligula are creatures of reason and will, whose encounters with the absurd are pure and clear. Meursault is a noble savage, untouched by religious consciousness. He lives as Rousseau imagined men before society, in amoral oneness with nature; it is the murder that brings him into the painful awareness of his duality, wherein Rousseau located both the source of corruption and the sole chance for moral existence, the one thing that elevates humans above the natural world.

In his final years, Camus the pagan had adopted a form of perception that was profoundly indebted to the Judeo-Christian tradition. Without abandoning the fundamental concept of his thought, the experience of the absurd, he enriched his vision by acknowledging human nature to be murkier than before. Not only good and evil are problematic, but even simplicity and sincerity. Meursault's refusal to lie is just another form of lie, and a self-deception first of all. There is a kind of Fall involved, mythical in human nature, but real and historical in Camus's thought, and transformed by his art into the masterpiece *The Fall*.

In explaining the greatness of *The Fall*, René Girard has written that the novel "is nothing other than the critical re-organization of past themes in terms of doubles. The critical force of the rupture is nothing but the doubles becoming explicit, the writer himself taking charge of them".[13] This process continues throughout *Exile and the Kingdom*, most openly in *The Renegade* and *The Growing Stone*, which I have discussed in terms of doubles and sacred monsters, but also to a significant degree in the other stories. Camus's biblical sources, the Adulterous Woman, Cain, and Jonah, are all involved in the drama of the sacrificial victim. Even *The Silent Men*, although lacking any biblical reference, evokes the myth of the scapegoat; for it is the arbitrary sacrifice of the innocent girl, Lassalle's daughter, that restores the original sense of community to the cooperage.

The mere presence of a theme does not, of course, argue strongly for the greatness of a work. Rather, it is Camus's originality, shared with only a few of the greatest writers, in refusing to collude in the ritual of sacrifice, once the province of religion, but which Girard claims has become in our times the function of literature more than of religion. The ritual repeats, while concealing, society's origin in violence. The differentiations that established a society's hierarchies are sanctified. In most literature, as in a religious ritual, the reader-celebrant undergoes the experience of trial so as to emerge reassured about the rightness of a certain order.

For Camus, in his last works, it became urgent to denounce the very differentiations he had advocated in the beginning. The judge, the priest, and the missionary are all doubles of the author and the reader; and Camus, as Girard puts it, takes charge of them. It is a constant of Camus's life work that he sought to reveal truths, however painful, about the human condition. When the quest for truth led him to the realization that he himself was the monster, the designated victim of the sacrifice, he did not shrink from the implications of the discovery. Both Clamence and Jonas are in part confessional self-portraits of the artist as villain, that is, as hypocrite and parasite. For the sake of society, such villains must be exposed.

They are also, like all monsters, our doubles. If Camus were content to denounce and expel the evil, he would simply be reinstituting the old order with a new personnel. The magnitude of the rupture with the past for Camus lies in his bold gaze into the abyss of that infinite regression; the fall is endless from the posture of rectitude. Tarrou, in *The Plague*, had illustrated the dilemma in practical terms; there seems to be no way not to bring evil into the world. Yet Tarrou is a kind of double to Father Paneloux, and both men seem to live, and die, in unison with the rise and decline of the plague itself. Their absolutism, even in a mode as noble as Tarrou's, seems to be another form of the evil. In *The Fall*, Camus goes another step and accepts the dilemma as his own; and in *Exile and the Kindom*, he begins working toward some other resolution than a perpetual re-sacralization of violence in new guises. The death sentence on Paneloux and Tarrou is not an adequate answer.

For that reason, the stories of *Exile and the Kingdom* do not move toward a conventional closure, but try instead to transfer their conflicts to the reader. In order to transcend violence, we must first acknowledge its pervasive presence in our thought. The stories engage the reader's complicity in some act of ritual violence, typically a critical judgment, only to force upon us afterward the realization of what we have done. Like the dancers of Iguape, we are hypnotized and swept along by the sensual flow of Camus's prose, and then awaken to the heavy burden of responsibility we must carry.

Most of the stories conclude bleakly, as if the only moral solution were self-immolation. A willed acceptance of the role of victim can, to be sure, transform its significance. In *The Growing Stone*, however, Camus seems to have hinted at a greater hope, that people could be happy even knowing the truth about existence, that is, without the comfortable illusions of a social order founded on violence. D'Arrast does not achieve happiness alone; the people of Iguape prove to be capable of understanding and sharing his gesture of transcendance, and, indeed, their simple faith teaches him something, too. The miracles, vows, processions, and the good Jesus may all be fictions; but so is any human account of the universe. The most important element of the Cook's faith is that it requires no lies; the Cook can admit that his prayers are not always answered. Moreover, he can appreciate the response of a nonbeliever like D'Arrast and accept his reinterpretation of the vow. In such a context, even religious faith and courtroom justice may help one realize the highest aspirations of Camus's morality: a perfect lucidity about one's relations with the universe; honesty in one's relations with other people; and solidarity with other human beings, based on respect for their freedom and awareness of a common fate. When, as occasionally happens, the lonely Camusian hero is surrounded by others who share those ideals, there occurs a transfiguring moment of human happiness. Such moments are the reward for a life well lived, and they are enough.

1. In "Camus's Stranger Retried."

2. A textbook edition, edited by Germaine Brée and Carlos Lynes, Jr., pp. vii–viii. Camus dated his "Avant-propos" 8 January 1955.

3. "est condamné parce qu'il ne joue pas le jeu . . . il refuse de mentir."

4. "Dans notre société tout homme qui ne pleure pas à l'enterrement de sa mère risque d'être condamné à mort."

5. "le seul Christ que nous méritions."

6. "paradoxalement."

7. In "Camus's *L'Etranger* Revisited."

8. See also the same critic's recent "Le Paradigme herméneutique chez Camus."

9. See also Alfred Noyer-Weidner, "Structure et sens de *L'Etranger*."

10. "J'ai eu l'impression bizarre d'être regardé par moi-même."

11. See Carl Viggiani, "Fall and Exile: Camus 1956–1958," especially pp. 272–75, for a recent discussion of Camus's attitude toward Christianity. Viggiani says almost nothing about *Exile and the Kingdom*, however.

12. Elwyn F. Sterling, "A Story of Cain: Another Look at 'l'Hôte.'"

13. *"To Double Business Bound"*, p. 42

Appendix: The English Translation of
L'Exil et le royaume

Justin O'Brien's translation of *Exile and the Kingdom* is extremely well done.[1] It conveys the meaning with great clarity, accuracy, and readability, and also preserves many of the other qualities of Camus's style. Inevitably, however, there are places where something has to be sacrificed; English and French are not identical languages. In discussing the stories, I have based all my remarks on the original French version, commenting on discrepancies or lost nuances in the English whenever necessary.[2] For the convenience of English-speaking readers, I have listed in this appendix all the cases where it seemed to me that a notable difference existed between the two texts. Only a very few of these could be termed mistranslations; most of the time, literal accuracy has been subordinated to some other important quality, or vice versa.[3]

The Adulterous Woman

"A housefly" (3); "Une mouche maigre" (1557). "House" is a precision not in the original, and the epithet "maigre"—"meager," "skinny," "skimpy," or perhaps "frail"—is omitted. The detail has some value because of Camus's use of contrasting sizes in this story.

"splattered with the dark-red spots of peppers" (22); "ensanglantées par les taches rouge sombre des piments" (1567). The French word actually means "blood-spattered."

"the sky above her was moving in a sort of slow gyration" (32); "une sorte de giration pesante entraînait le ciel au-dessus d'elle" (1572). Camus insists on the theme of weight; "slow" for "pesante" weakens this allusion. Recasting the sentence so as to make the sky the subject rather than the object similarly reduces the force of the image, which is based on gravity.

"the dead weight of others" (32); "le poids des êtres" (1572). The French is literally "the weight of beings."

"turned on the light, which blinded her" (33); "donna la lumière qui la gifla en plein visage" (1573). The French image is more striking than the English: "which slapped her right in the face."

The Renegade

"The Renegade" (34); *"Le Renégat, ou un esprit confus"* (1577). The subtitle "or a confused mind" has been omitted in English.

"then it all begins again—oh, I hear too many things" (34); "puis tout recommence, ô j'entends trop de choses" (1577). This illustrates a change in punctuation typical of the English version; more than a dozen such dashes have been added to clarify the syntax.

"Fetish, Sorcerer, House of the Fetish" (passim); none of these terms is capitalized in the French.

"gra"; "râ" (passim). The meaning of this interjection is a subject of debate. As an initial syllable in French, it seems to be associated with harshness, in words like "railler, râle, râpe," that is, "mock, death rattle, rasp." The rather arbitrary use of a circumflex accent gives the word an exotic air, and lends some credibility to the suggestion that it is meant to invoke the sun god Ra.[4]

"What a jumble"; "Quelle bouillie" (passim). The translation preserves the primary meaning faithfully enough, but some of the connotations of the French term are lost. The etymological sense of the word is "boiled," which is appropriate to the pervasive heat of the desert. In idiomatic usage, "mettre en bouillie" means "beat to a pulp," and "bouillie pour les chats" means "unreadable text"; both have relevance in this story.

"it seems" (34); "je ne sais pas" (1577). Like the other small modifications in this story, this tends to make the English clearer than the French.

"Order and method" (34); "De l'ordre, un ordre" (1577). The English avoids the repetition unnecessarily, and possibly alters the significance of the movement from order in general to *an* order, one among many.

"this country drives men mad and I've been here I don't know how many years" (34); "cette terre rend fou et moi, depuis tant d'années que je n'en sais plus le compte" (1577). "I've been here" is interpolated.

"Grenoble's hot sun" (36); "le soleil de Grenoble" (1578). "the blinding sun" (38); "le soleil torride" (1579). "the blinding scales" (42); "écailles éblouissantes' (1581). "dazzling whiteness" (42); "blancheur fulgurante" (1581). In the first phrase, "hot" is interpolated; in the second, "hot" or "torrid" would be more accurate, and in the third, "dazzling" would be closer to the original, and "withering" would be more precise in the fourth. Individually not very important, together these small differences vary significantly from the original, especially because blindness is mentioned by Camus.

"pig-headed"; "mulet, tête dure" (passim). "pig of a father" (36); "mon père ce porc" (1578). Camus compares the son to a mule, and "porc" suggests swinishness rather than stubbornness.

"I have something to settle with him and with his teachers, with my teachers who deceived me" (36); "J'ai un compte à régler avec lui et avec ses maîtres, avec mes maîtres qui m'ont trompé" (1578). The secondary meaning "master" is very present in the French.

"the greatest of masters" (36); "le plus grand des seigneurs" (1578). Here the French term means "lord," and is used in the same passage capitalized: "le Seigneur," "the Lord."

"give credit" (36); "rendre hommage" (1578). The French is a metaphor, "pay homage," which sustains the implications of the term "lord."

"the children's teeth are set on edge" (36); "leurs enfants ont des dents cariées" (1587). The meaning is rather that the children have decayed teeth.

"I went out of my way for punishments, I groused at the normal" (37); "j'allais au-devant des pénitences, je rognais sur l'ordinaire" (1678). The second part of the sentence actually means "I cut back on my regular allotment of food."

"I'd get the upper hand of those savages like a strong sun. Strong, yes, that was the word I constantly had on the tip of my tongue, I dreamed of absolute power" (39); "je subjuguerais ces sauvages, comme un soleil puissant. Puissant, oui, c'était le mot que sans cesse, je roulais sur ma langue je rêvais du pouvoir absolu" (1579). "Subjugate" is the literal and cognate meaning of the first verb. "Puissant" is etymologically linked to "pouvoir," a connection not shown in the English "strong" and "power."

"They'll show you" (41); "ils t'apprendront" (1580). The more literal "they"ll teach you" would preserve the relationship to the Renegade's seminary teachers or masters.

"I was going blind" (42); "je devenais aveugle" (1581). The habitual rather than the progressive would be more accurate in English: "I would go blind [at such times]."

"Just one rain, Lord! But what do I mean, what Lord, they are the lords and masters! They rule over their sterile homes" (43); "Une seule pluie, Seigneur! Mais quoi, quel seigneur, ce sont eux les seigneurs! Ils règnent sur leurs maisons stériles" (1581). The capital letter makes "Seigneur" or "Lord" refer to the Christian God. The Renegade lapses here momentarily in thinking of Him, but immediately corrects himself and then reveals the extent of his apostasy by confusing God with the men of Taghâsa. The English, by capitalizing the second "Lord" and adding the word "masters" makes this subtle point less clear.

"a wicked hope consumes me" (51); "un espoir méchant me brûle" (1586). The French verb means "burn"; once again, an allusion to the heat is lost.

"madness took away my tongue" (51); "la folie m'a pris à la langue" (1586). A more accurate rendering would be "went to my tongue" or "took me by the tongue." In the same paragraph, the word "silence" is omitted from the enumeration "Not a bird, not a blade of grass, stone, an arid desire, silence, their screams,"

"a heaven moved to pity" (59); "le ciel qui s'attendrit" (1590). The French has both this meaning and a more physical one, "a softening sky."

This story, stylistically the most remarkable in the collection, perhaps for that very reason presents far more problems in the translation than any other. It is the only one where the English version may be said to diverge consistently in one direction, making the Renegade's inner monolog a bit more lucid than it was written by Camus, and weakening a few of the extended images.

The Silent Men

"cycling slowly" (62); "roulait lourdement" (1595). "got up slowly" (75); "se leva pesamment" (1602). Both French adverbs mean "heavily."

"in a wheelchair" (63); "aux allongés" (1595). The French is a jocular phrase for "among the dead."

"The union had to consider the other cooper's shops that hadn't gone along. You couldn't really blame the union" (65); "Le syndicat tenait compte des autres tonnelleries qui n'avaient pas marché. On ne pouvait pas trop leur en vouloir" (1596). The French plural pronoun indicates that Yvars could not blame the other shops, rather than the union.

"He [Lassalle] had forced the union's hand" (67); "Ils avaient forcé la main au syndicat" (1597). The French subject is plural; the workers themselves had forced the union's hand.

"calamity" (81); "malheur" (1605). "Misfortune" would be the usual translation, and better preserves the implication that fate is to blame.

The Guest

The title poses an impossible problem, since the French word "hôte" can mean either "host" or "guest," and the ambiguity about which is which is an important theme in the story.

"fought bitterly" (98); "se mordaient à la gorge" (1615). The French contains a discreet allusion to the Arab's actual crime, cutting a man's throat; literally it means "bit each other in the throat."

The Artist at Work

The title once again poses a problem. In French, it is "Jonas, ou l'artiste au travail." The English has retained only the subtitle, quite possibly because the name "Jonas" can mean either "Jonas" or "Jonah."

"he poses as wicked or ugly" (115); "il se veut méchant ou laid" (1629). The French means literally "he wills himself," and is part of a mild satire of existentialism.

"as you say"; "comme vous voudrez" (passim). Here again, the French verb expresses a will. This time the joke is on Jonas, who alternates between this cliché and "What luck!"

"constantly changing moods of the internal-revenue office" (116); "dispositions sans cesse renouvelées de la fiscalité" (1630). The term "dispositions" is a pun, meaning both "moods" and "legal provisions."

The Growing Stone

"jetty"; "digue" (passim). The cognate "dike" or "levee" or "embankment" would seem more appropriate to the apparent function, which is to keep the river from flooding the town.

"urubu"; "urubu" (passim). It is a vulture.

"clumsily" (159); "lourdement" (1655). "solidly" (160); "lourdement" (1655). "intensified" (161); "alourdissait" (1656). "the slapping of the water" (164); "le clapotis des eaux lourdes" (1658). "the harsh sun" (167); "le soleil lourd" (1659). As in some of the other stories, Camus's obsessive use of terms related to heaviness has not been carried over into English.

"each time he came back to life" (161); "à chaque résurrection" (1656). This is a metaphorical description of D'Arrast in the flashing headlights; the French term more explicitly suggests the religious analogy.

"Have no fear" (171); "Sois pas peur" (1661). The English is correct and even a bit elegant; the French is pidgin French. In this story, the problem of rendering the languages is no doubt insoluble. At times we would be reading the English translation of a conventional French rendering of Spanish spoken by native Portuguese speakers. This theme could be studied only by someone capable of reading the original.

"pea-jacket" (181); "vareuse marinière" (1667). A pea-jacket is too heavy for the climate.

"Noble" (182); "seigneur" (1668). Again, the possible fusion of the social, political, and religious images is not retained in the English, as it might have been with "lord."

"'You like to dance?' 'Oh, yes! I like'" (184). Between D'Arrast's question and the Cook's reply, a descriptive line has been omitted: "Les yeux du coq brillèrent d'une sorte de gourmandise" (1669), that is, the "The Cook's eyes shone with a sort of greediness."

---

1. See the Bibliography for details of the editions used. In this appendix, references to both the English and the French texts will be given in the text in parentheses.

2. Obviously, I assume that Camus's text is the valid one, which implies belief in, and respect for, his intentions. I admit that I have both, in full awareness of the problematic status of authorial intentionality. Some contemporary theories of literature, emphasizing the production of meaning through the reader's interplay with the text, might challenge that assumption, or at least insist on its arbitrariness, even with regard to translations. An interesting commentary on the theoretical problems of translation, based on German translations of Camus, can be found in Fritz Paepcke's "Albert Camus en traduction."

3. There is certainly nothing to justify the kinds of criticism that have been leveled at Stuart Gilbert's translation of *L'Etranger*. See John Gale, "Does America Know *The Stranger*?", and Helen Sebba, "Stuart Gilbert's Meursault: A Strange Stranger."

4. See Stephen Ullmann, *The Image in the Modern French Novel*, p. 293, and Cryle, *Bilan*, p. 99. The French write both "Râ" and "Rè," although the latter is more common.

Bibliography

Works by Camus

Exile and the Kingdom. Trans. Justin O'Brien. New York: Alfred A.
  Knopf, 1958. The Vintage paperback edition has the same pagination.
  The Adulterous Woman, pp. 3–33;
  The Renegade, pp. 34–61;
  The Silent Men, pp. 62–84;
  The Guest, pp. 85–109;
  The Artist at Work, pp. 110–58
  The Growing Stone, pp. 159–213.

The Fall. Trans. Justin O'Brien. New York: Alfred A. Knopf, 1956. The Vintage
paperback edition has the same pagination.

Théâtre, Récits, Nouvelles. Ed. Roger Quilliot. "Bibliothèque de la Pléiade" no. 161.
Paris: Gallimard. The date 1962, cited on the verso of the title page, is that of the
copyright. The edition I have used was printed in 1963, a date cited on the verso of the
half-title page preceding the title page. Users of the edition printed in 1981, a date cited
on the flyleaf facing p. 2088, should add 2 to every page number. Although nothing on
the title page or in the introductory material identifies the later printing as a revised
edition, it can be recognized by the fact that it has 2088 rather than 2082 pages. The
prefatory material to *La Dévotion à la croix*, on p. 526 of the 1963 edition, is spread
over pp. 526–28 of the 1981 edition; this change accounts for the two-page displace-
ment of *L'Exil et le royaume*. A text entitled "Emission de Renée Saurel" has been
added on pp. 1747–50. The outline biography on pp. xxvii–xxxvii has also been
reworked. The stories are found on the following pages in the 1963 edition (the 1981
edition in parentheses):
  La Femme adultère, pp. 1557–73 (1559–75);
  Le Renégat, ou un esprit confus, pp. 1577–91 (1579–93)
  Les Muets, pp. 1595–1606 (1597–1608);
  L'Hôte, pp. 1609–21 (1611–23);
  Jonas, ou l'artiste au travail, pp. 1627–52 (1629–54)
  La Pierre qui pousse, pp. 1655–84 (1657–86).

Other Works Consulted

Abbou, André, Salomon Malka, and Gérard Spitéri. "Albert Camus vingt ans après." *Nouvelles Littéraires*, 10–17 January 1980, pp. 18–19.

Abel, Lionel. "Seven Heroes of the New Left." *New York Times Magazine*, 5 May 1968, pp. 30 ff.

"Action-Packed Intellectual." *Life*, 14 October 1957, p. 125–28.

"Albert Camus." Editorial, *New York Times*, 5 January 1960, p. 30; article on his death pp. 1, 4.

"Albert Camus Wins Nobel Letters Prize." *New York Times*, 18 October 1957, pp. 1, 8.

Archambault, Paul. "Albert Camus et la métaphysique chrétienne." In Gay-Crosier, *Albert Camus 1980*, pp. 210–20.

Bailey, Anthony. "The Isolated Man." *Commonweal*, 25 October 1957, pp. 91–93.

Balakian, Anna. "Alienation and Aridity: The Climatic Correlative in Camus's Writings." In Zyla and Aycock, pp. 37–52.

Bartfeld, Fernande. *Camus et Hugo.* "Archives Albert Camus No. 3." Paris: Archives des Lettres Modernes, 1975.

———. "Les Paradoxes du *Jonas* de Camus." *Hebrew University Studies in Literature* 6 (1978): 129–42.

Braun, Lev. *Witness of Decline: Albert Camus, Moralist of the Absurd.* Rutherford, N.J.: Fairleigh Dickinson University Press, 1974.

Brée, Germaine. *Camus.* New Brunswick, N.J.: Rutgers University Press, 1961.

———, ed. *Camus: A Collection of Critical Essays.* Englewood Cliffs, N.J.: Prentice-Hall, 1962.

Brody, Jules. "Camus et la pensée tragique: *L'Etranger.*" *Saggi e Ricerche di Letteratura Francese* (1976): 511–54.

Brombert, Victor. *The Intellectual Hero: Studies in the French Novel 1880–1955.* London: Faber and Faber, 1961.

Brooks, Cleanth, and Robert Penn Warren. *Understanding Fiction.* 2d ed. New York: Appleton-Century-Crofts, 1959.

Charlton, D. G., ed. *France: A Companion to French Studies.* New York: Pitman Publishing Corp., 1972

Claire, Thomas. "Landscape and Religious Imagery in Camus's *La Pierre qui pousse.*" *Studies in Short Fiction* 13 (1976): 321–29.

Costes, Alain. *Albert Camus, ou la parole manquante, étude psychnalytique.* Paris: Payot, 1973.

Cruickshank, John. *Albert Camus and the Literature of Revolt.* London: Oxford University Press, 1959.

———. "French Literature since 1870." In Charlton, pp. 385–437.

———. *The Novelist as Philosopher.* London: Oxford University Press, 1962.

Cryle, Peter. *Bilan critique: "L'Exil et le royaume" d'Albert Camus, essai d'analyse.* Paris: Lettres Modernes, Minard, 1973.

———. "The Written Painting and the Painted Word in *Jonas.*" In Gay-Crosier, *Albert Camus 1980*, pp. 123–32.

Curtis, Jerry L. "Alienation and the Foreigner in *Exile and the Kingdom.*" *French Literature Series* 2 (1975): 127–38.

———. "Structure and Space in Camus's *Jonas.*" *Modern Fiction Studies* 22 (1976–77): 571–76.

Davis, Richard Gorham. "Exploration into the Guilt of Man." Review of *The Fall. New York Times Book Review*, 17 February 1957, pp. 1ff.

———. "Faith for an Age without Faith." Review of *Exile and the Kingdom. New York Times Book Review*, 9 March 1958, pp. 1ff.

Durand, Laura G. "Thematic Counterpoint in *L'Exil et le royaume.*" *French Review* 47 (1974): 1110–22.

Fitch, Brian T. "Camus's Desert Hieroglyphics." In Zyla and Aycock, pp. 117–31.

———. *"L'Etranger" d'Albert Camus.* Paris: Larousse, 1972.

———. *"Jonas* ou la production d'une étoile." *Albert Camus* 6. *Revue des Lettres Modernes* 360–65 (1973): 51–65.

———. "Le Paradigme herméneutique chez Camus." In Gay-Crosier, *Albert Camus 1980*, pp. 32–48.

———, and Peter C. Hoy. "Bibliographie des études comparatives." *Albert Camus* 4. *Revue des Lettres Modernes* 264–70 (1971): 287–323.

Flanner, Janet ("Genêt"). "Letter from Paris." *New Yorker*, 2 November 1957, pp. 146–50.

———. "Letter from Paris." *New Yorker*, 6 February 1965, pp. 115–16.

Fletcher, Dennis. "Camus between Yes and No: A Fresh Look at the Murder in *L'Etranger.*" *Neophilologus* 61 (1977): 523–33.

Fortier, Paul A. "Création et fonctionnement de l'atmosphère dans *Le Renégat* d'Albert Camus." *PMLA* (1973): 484–95. English Translation in Suther, pp. 217–45.

———. "Le Décor symbolique de *L'Hôte* d'Albert Camus." *French Review* 46 (1973): 535–42. English translation in Suther, pp. 203–15.

———. *Une Lecture de Camus: La Valeur des éléments descriptifs dans l'oeuvre romanesque.* Paris: Klincksieck, 1977.

Gadourek, Carina. *Les Innocents et les coupables: essai d'exégèse de l'oeuvre d'Albert Camus.* La Haye: Mouton, 1963.

Gale, John. "Does America Know *The Stranger*? A Reappraisal of a Translation." *Modern Fiction Studies* 20 (1974): 139–47.

Gay-Crosier, Raymond, ed. *Albert Camus 1980.* Gainesville: University Presses of Florida, 1980.

———. *Les Envers d'un échec: étude sur le théâtre d'Albert Camus.* Paris: Lettres Modernes, Minard, 1967.

Gélinas, Germain-Paul. *La Liberté dans la pensée d'Albert Camus.* Fribourg Switzerland: Editions Universitaires, 1965.

"Genêt." See Flanner, Janet.

Girard, René. "Camus's Stranger Retried." *PMLA* 79 (1964): 519–33. Reprinted in *"To Double Business Bound"*, pp. 9–35.

————. "*To Double Business Bound*". Baltimore: Johns Hopkins University Press, 1978.

————. *La Violence et le sacré*. Paris: Bernard Grasset, 1972.

Goldstain, Jacques. "Camus et la Bible." *Albert Camus* 4. *Revue des Lettres Modernes* 264-70 (1971): 97-140.

Grobe, Edwin P. "The Psychological Structure of Camus's *L'Hôte*." *French Review* 40 (1966): pp. 357-76.

Guthrie, Ramon. "Six Camus Experiments in a New Medium." Review of *Exile and the Kingdom*. *New York Herald-Tribune Book Review*, 9 March 1958, p. 3.

Haig, Stirling. "The Epilogue of *Crime and Punishment* and Camus's *La Femme Adultère*." *Comparative Literature Studies* 3 (1966): 445-49.

Hartmann, Geoffrey. "Camus and Malraux: The Common Ground." *Yale French Studies* 25, *Albert Camus* (1960): pp. 104-10.

Hermet, Joseph. *Albert Camus et le christianisme*. Paris: Beauchesne, 1976.

Hoy, Peter C. *Camus in English*. Paris: Lettres Modernes, Minard, 1971.

Hutcheon, Linda. "*Le Renégat, ou un esprit confus* comme nouveau récit." *Albert Camus* 6. *Revue des Lettres Modernes* 360-65 (1973): 69-87. English translation in Suther, pp. 259-78.

Ingram, Forrest L. *Representative Short Story Cycles of the Twentieth Century*. La Haye: Mouton, 1971.

Issacharoff, Michael. *L'Espace et la nouvelle: Flaubert, Huysmans, Ionesco, Sartre, Camus*. Paris: Corti, 1976.

————. "Le Mythe solaire chez Camus." *Francité* 1 (1972): 87-98.

————. "Une Symbolique de l'espace: lecture de *La Pierre qui pousse* d'Albert Camus." *Cahiers de l'Association Internationale des Etudes Françaises* 27 (1975): 255-72.

Joiner, Lawrence D. "Camus's *Le Renégat*: Identity Denied." *Studies in Short Fiction* 13 (1976): 37-41.

————. "Camus's *The Renegade*: A Quest for Sexual Identity." *Research Studies* 45 (1977): 171-76.

————. "Reverie and Silence in *Le Renégat*." *Romance Notes* 16 (1975): 262-67.

Kanfer, Stefan. "Camus: Normal Virtues in Abnormal Times." *Time*, 10 July 1978, pp. 74-75.

King, Adele. *Camus*. London: Oliver and Boyd, 1964.

————. "*Jonas, ou l'artiste au travail*." *French Studies* 20 (1966): 267-80.

Knopf, Blanche. "Albert Camus in the Sun." *Atlantic Monthly*, February 1961, pp. 77-84.

Lamont, Rosette. "The Anti-Bourgeois." *French Review* 34 (1961): 445-53.

Lévi-Valensi, Jacqueline. *Les Critiques de notre temps et Camus*. Paris: Garnier, 1970.

Lottman, Herbert R. *Albert Camus, a Biography*. New York: Doubleday, 1979.

Mason, Haydn T. "Voltaire and Camus." *Romanic Review* 59 (1968): pp. 198-212.

McCarthy, Patrick. *Camus: A Critical Study of his Life and Work*. London: Hamish Hamilton, 1982.

Merwin, W. S. "Through the Blur of Pain." Review of *Exile and the Kingdom*. *Nation*, 16 August 1958, pp. 74-75.

Miles, O. Thomas. "Three Authors in Search of a Character." *Personalist* 46 (1965): 65–72.

Miller, Owen J. "*L'Exil et le royaume*: cohérence du recueil." *Albert Camus* 6. *Revue des Lettres Modernes* 160–65 (1973): 21–50.

Miller, Stephen. "The Posthumous Victory of Albert Camus. *Commentary*, November 1980, pp. 53–58.

Minor, Anne. "The Short Stories of Albert Camus." *Yale French Studies* 25, *Albert Camus* (1970): 75–80.

Moeller, Charles. "Albert Camus: The Question of Hope." *Cross Currents* 8 (1958): pp. 172–84.

Molnar, Thomas. "Albert Camus: Guide of a Generation." *Catholic World*, January 1958, pp. 272–77.

———. "Camus, Voice of a Searching Generation." *Catholic World*, May 1960, pp. 94–96 ff.

Murchland, Bernard G. "Albert Camus: Rebel." *Catholic World*, January 1959, pp. 308–14.

———. "Between Solitude and Solidarity." *Commonweal*, 23 October 1970, pp. 91–95.

———. "One Step Further on a Solitary Way." Review of *Exile and the Kingdom*. *Commonweal*, 28 March 1958, pp. 663–64.

Nguyen-Van-Huy, Pierre. *La Métaphysique du bonheur chez Albert Camus*. Neuchâtel: La Baconière, 1962.

Nicolas, André. *Albert Camus, ou le vrai Prométhée*. Paris: Seghers, 1966.

"Nobel Prize Winner." Editorial. *New York Times*, 19 October 1957, p. 20.

Noyer-Weidner, Alfred. "Albert Camus im Stadium der Novelle (*L'Exil et le royaume*)." *Zeitschrift für französische Sprache und Literatur* 70 (1960): 1–38. English Translation in Suther, pp. 45–87.

———. "Structure et sens de *L'Etranger*." In Gay-Crosier, *Albert Camus 1980*, pp. 72–86.

O'Brien, Conor Cruise. "The Angel of the Absurd." Review of McCarthy, *Camus*. *TLS*, 7 May 1982, p. 505.

O'Brien, Justin. "An Entry in Camus's Bibliography." Review of *Albert Camus: The Invincible Summer*, by Albert Maquet. *New York Times Book Review*, 5 January 1958, p. 14.

———, and Leon S. Roudiez. "Camus." *Saturday Review*, 13 February 1960, pp. 19–21 ff.

Onimus, Jean. *Camus*. Paris: Desclée de Brouwer, 1965.

Paepcke, Fritz. "Albert Camus en traduction." In Gay-Crosier, *Albert Camus 1980*, pp. 15–31.

Pelz, Manfred. *Die Novellen von Albert Camus*. Freiburg: Universitätsverlag Becksmann, 1973.

Peters, Renate. "L'Art, la révolte, et l'histoire: *Le Renégat* et *L'Homme révolté*." *French Review* 54 (1981): 517–23.

Picon, Gaëton. "*Exile and the Kingdom*." In Brée, ed., *Camus: A Collection of Critical Essays*, pp. 152–56.

————. "Mercuriale. Lettres. *L'Exil et le Royaume*." *Mercure de France*, May 1957, pp. 127–31.

Podhoretz, Norman. "Solitary or Solidary?" Review of *Exile and the Kingdom*. *New Yorker*, 29 March 1958, pp. 115–22.

Prescott, Orville. "Books of the Times: *Exile and the Kingdom*." *New York Times*, 10 March 1958, p. 21.

————. "Books of the Times: *The Fall*." *New York Times*, 18 February 1957, p. 25.

"A Questioning Voice Is Stilled." *Christian Century*, 20 January 1960, p. 67–68.

Quilliot, Roger. "Un Monde ambigu." In Lévi-Valensi, pp. 98–100.

————. See Camus, *Théâtre, Récits, Nouvelles*.

Rauhut, F. "Du nihilisme à la 'mesure' et à l'amour des *hommes*." In Thieberger, pp. 17–40.

Reck, Rima Drell. "Albert Camus: The Artist and his Time." *Modern Language Quarterly* 23 (1962): pp. 129–34.

Redfern, W. D. "Camus and Confusion." *Symposium* 20 (1966):

Rizzuto, Anthony. *Camus' Imperial Vision*. Carbondale: Southern Illinois University Press, 1981.

Roelens, Maurice. "Un Texte, son histoire, et l'histoire: *L'Hôte* d'Albert Camus." *Revue des Sciences Humaines* 165 (1977): 5–22.

Rolo, Charles. "Albert Camus, a Good Man." *Atlantic Monthly*, May 1958, pp. 27–33.

Rooke, Constance. "Camus's *The Guest*." *Studies in Short Fiction* 14 (1977): 78–81.

Sebba, Helen. "Stuart Gilbert's Meursault: A Strange 'Stranger.'" *Contemporary Literature* 13 (1972): pp. 334–40.

Showalter, English. "Camus's Mysterious Guests: A Note on the Value of Ambiguity." *Studies in Short Fiction* 4 (1966): 348–50.

"Six from Camus." Review of *Exile and the Kingdom*. *Time*, 17 March 1958, p. 111.

Solotaroff, Theodore. "Camus's Portable Pedestal." *New Republic*, 21 December 1968, pp. 27–30.

Stancioff, Marion Mitchell. "Camus: Solitary or Solidary?" *America*, 4 January 1958, pp. 395–97.

"The Startled Winner." *Newsweek*, 28 October 1957, pp. 50–51.

Sterling, Elwyn F. "A Story of Cain: Another Look at *L'Hôte*." *French Review* 54 (1981): 524–29.

Suther, Judith D., ed. *Essays on Camus's "Exile and the Kingdom."* University, Miss.: Romance Monographs, 1980.

Thieberger, Richard, ed. *Configuration critique d'Albert Camus* 2: *Camus devant la critique allemande*. *Revue des Lettres Modernes* 90–93 (1963).

Thody, Philip. *Albert Camus, 1913–1960*. London: Hamilton, 1961.

————. "Anguish of Life." Review of *Exile and the Kingdom*. *Saturday Review*, 15 March 1958, p. 23.

————. "Camus's *L'Etranger* Revisited." *Critical Quarterly* 22 no. 2 (1979): 61–69.

Treil, Claude. *L'Indifférence dans l'oeuvre de Camus*. Sherbrooke, Quebec: Editions Cosmos; Paris: Nizet, 1971.

Ullmann, Stephen. *The Image in the Modern French Novel: Gide, Alain-Fournier, Proust, Camus*. Cambridge: At the University Press, 1960.

Viggiani, Carl. "Fall and Exile: Camus 1956–1958." In Gay-Crosier, *Albert Camus 1980*, pp. 269–76.

Womack, William R., and F. S. Heck. "A Note on Camus's *The Guest*." *International Fiction Review* 2 (1975): 163–65.

Zahareas, Anthony. "*La Femme adultère*: Camus's Ironic Vision of the Absurd." *Texas Studies in Literature and Language* 5 (1963): 319–28.

Zants, Emily. "Camus's Deserts and their Allies, Kingdoms of the Stranger." *Symposium* 17 (1963): 30–41.

Zyla, Wolodymyr T., and Wendell M. Aycock, eds. *Proceedings of the Comparative Literature Symposium (Texas Tech) 8: Albert Camus's Literary Milieu: Arid Lands*. Lubbock: Texas Tech Press, 1976.

Index

Abel, Lionel, 7
Adulterous Woman, the (biblical version), 25–29
Adulterous Woman, The. See Camus: *The Adulterous Woman*
Algeria, 4, 12, 14, 75–78, 84, 131
Algeria, as setting, 22, 75–78, 99–100, 102, 108
Amsterdam, 92, 101, 140
Arab prisoner (*The Guest*), 73–87, 110, 118, 125, 129, 138
Arabs, 22, 24, 30, 57, 61, 63, 66–67, 73–87, 132
Archives des Lettres Modernes, 3
Artist at Work, The (painting), 96, 104
Artist at Work, The. See Camus: *The Artist at Work*
Aury, Dominique, 90

Balducci (*The Guest*), 75, 77, 79–80, 82–83, 85, 110, 123, 126
Ballester (*The Silent Men*), 62, 83
Balzac, Honoré de, 95, 132
Bartfeld, Fernande, 96
Barthes, Roland, 9
Beckett, Samuel, 35
Beffort (*The Renegade*), 36, 39, 44, 52
Bergman, Ingmar, 66
Bible, the, 25–29, 90, 93, 140–41
Brazil, 12, 57, 61, 107–8, 115, 119, 121–22, 127
Brody, Jules, 132–33
Brombert, Victor, 43–44

Brooks, Cleanth, 7

Camus, Albert:
—Works by
  Cain, 140–41
  Caligula, 43, 140
  Exile and the Kingdom, 5–8, 10, 14–15, 47–48, 54, 65, 95, 125, 131, 134–36, 140–42
  Adulterous Woman, The, 5, 7, 11, 15, 19–34, 47–48, 55, 57, 59, 61, 63, 66, 90, 119, 121, 134, 140–41, 145–46. *See also* Jackal-soldier; Janine; Marcel
  Artist at Work, The, 11–12, 15, 17, 35, 89–106, 107, 149. *See also* Jonas, Louise, Rateau
  Growing Stone, The, 5, 7, 11–13, 15, 55, 58, 107–29, 139–41, 143, 149–50. *See also* D'Arrast; Cook, the; Harbor Captain, the; Judge, the; Police Chief, the; Socrates
  Guest, The, 5, 7, 12, 15, 55, 57, 59, 73–87, 123, 137, 140, 149. *See also* Arab prisoner; Balducci, Daru
  Renegade, The, 5, 7, 15, 35–52, 57, 66, 69, 96, 134–35, 140–41, 146–48. *See also* Beffort; Renegade, the; Sorcerer, the
  Silent Men, The, 5, 11–12, 15, 30, 53–71, 80, 84, 122, 126, 140–41, 148–49. *See also* Ballester,